THE WORK OF THE NINTH DIVISION

THE WORK OF
THE NINTH DIVISION

BY

MAJOR-GENERAL SIR H. E. COLVILE,
K.C.M.G., C.B.

AUTHOR OF
'THE LAND OF THE NILE SPRINGS,' ETC.

The Naval & Military Press Ltd

in association with

The National Army Museum, London

Published jointly by

The Naval & Military Press Ltd
Unit 10 Ridgewood Industrial Park,
Uckfield, East Sussex,
TN22 5QE England

Tel: +44 (0) 1825 749494
Fax: +44 (0) 1825 765701

www.naval-military-press.com
www.military-genealogy.com
www.militarymaproom.com

and

The National Army Museum, London
www.national-army-museum.ac.uk

In reprinting in facsimile from the original, any imperfections are inevitably reproduced and the quality may fall short of modern type and cartographic standards.

FOREWORD

A DIVISION and its Commander are so closely linked that the fortune of one is the fortune of both. Together they share praise and rewards, together they bear blame and punishment. Thus, while it is to the splendid conduct of all ranks of the Ninth Division that I owe any credit I gained as its Commander, the shortness of its life and the obscurity that covers many of its deeds are due to certain decisions of mine. On me, therefore, rightly falls the task of dispelling the darkness which has fallen upon its past and making its brief history clear for the future.

It is no part of the scheme of this book to treat of the matters which have lately been discussed in Parliament, except in so far as they influenced the fate of the Division. This much, however, I may say: that had the events which were the immediate cause of that debate happened between the date on which the Army Act became law and the last month of 1900, a practicable appeal to the Sovereign, Head of the Army, would have been open to me*

* See Appendix III.

through another court than that which had condemned me, and such an appeal could only have been made complete by telling the work of the Ninth Division. After that date, however, there remained but two ways of making the story of that work known—namely, by publishing it either from behind the safe shelter of another writer or in my own name. Perhaps the former would have been the wiser course, but I think the latter the more straightforward one. If I am blamed for it, I trust, at all events, that any hostile feeling I may raise against myself will not bias the reader's judgment of the work of the Ninth Division.

H. E. COLVILE.

May 11, 1901.

CONTENTS

PROLOGUE

THE GUARDS BRIGADE

Appointment—Voyage out—Concentration—Night attacks—Belmont—Reconnaissance—The invisible hill—A soldiers' battle—Enslin—Kolke Liegte—Modder River—Riet in the way—Pom-pom—A trying day—A containing force—Methuen wounded—Magersfontein—A night march—The first fusillade—Rearguard—Cool hands—A dull six weeks - - - 1-17

CHAPTER I

THE PAARDEBERG MARCH

Appointment—Staff—Orders—First march—Concentration—First breakdown—Ramdam—A Boer homestead—Enteric—Waterval Drift—Night marches—A bad drift—A suitable escort—Wegdrai—Jacobsdal—A scare—Orders for march—A regrettable incident—A determined sentry—Klip Drift—A halt in the night—A short rest - - - - - 18-32

CHAPTER II

PAARDEBERG

Enemy advancing—Description of ground—Kelly-Kenny—Plans—A sudden flood—No pontoons—Orders—Battery recalled—Passage of the Modder—Nineteenth

Brigade—Highland Brigade—A fine advance—Attack formations—The critical point—The Cornwall's charge — Casualties — Creeping forward — Boer trenches—Smells—Advance of the Shropshires—The advanced trench—Expert opinion—Orders for the attack—The Canadians' night assault—A hard night's work—Surrender—Prisoners—Two sorts of pluck—Osfontein - - - - - - 33-52

CHAPTER III

POPLAR GROVE

Plans—Description of ground—Leeuwkop—Operation orders—Difficulties of pushing on—Highland Brigade weak—Seventh Division—Enemy retreating—Naval guns—Artillery fire—Mounted signallers—Hot coffee —The Nineteenth Brigade—The Shropshires' attack —General retirement—The captured gun—Recross the river—Kelly-Kenny's fight—Dreifontein—Doornboom—Ventersvlei—Fererra's Spruit—Mr. John Steyn—Bloemfontein—The lost Aide-de-Camp—Refitting - - - - - - 53-67

CHAPTER IV

SANNAH'S POST

Broadwood's retirement—Ninth Division to join him—A long march—A hot day—News at Springfield—Escort for guns—Fourteen miles an hour—View from Boesman's Kop—Waterval held by Martyr—Broadwood safe—Guns away—The problem—Cavalry wanted—Choice of roads—Advantages of Waterval—Arrival of Division—A serviceable force—A tempting route—Ruggles-Brise's report—Cavalry exhausted—The Division tailing—Lord Roberts' orders—A turning movement—Waterval Drift—The two commandos—No news of French—Too late—Value of the Water-

CONTENTS ix

PAGE

works—Removal of wounded—Red Cross—Back to Bloemfontein—Idle rumours - - - 68-93

CHAPTER V

BLOEMFONTEIN TO WINBURG

Defence of Bloemfontein—A Boer meeting—A secret—Cavalry orders—Rietfontein—Divisional cavalry—Loss of Ruggles-Brise—Move of the Nineteenth Brigade—Cross-purposes—Transport—Orders for a move—Further orders—In the wrong place—French's movements—The Waterworks—Operations—More Batteries—Highland Light Infantry to rejoin - 94-110

CHAPTER VI

BLOEMFONTEIN TO WINBURG—*continued*

Waterval again—Forward move—Hopes—Wants—Drafts—Eastern Province Horse—A hard week—A mistake—Too much Staff—Hamilton's orders—Our position—Hamilton's plans—Field telegraph—Babiaansberg—A strong position—The Black Watch—Clever handling—The kloof at the top—A good performance—A trap—Hamilton's convoy—Welkom Drift—Hamilton to push on—Convoy difficulties—Winburg—No need for hurry - - - 111-132

CHAPTER VII

WINBURG

A proposal—An awkward position—To garrison Winburg—Charity—Illness of Staff—The Landdrost—The first convoy—Broadwood's despatch—The lost patrol—Macdonald to Ventersburg—Signs of improvement—Orders for march—Yeomanry to join—The cipher telegram—The 'general idea'—The advance on the

Vaal—Supply difficulties—A march on full rations—More sickness—The 5th Battery—No clothes—A fair start - - - - - - 133-156

CHAPTER VIII

WINBURG TO LINDLEY

Zand River—Yeomanry not coming—Field Hospital—A man with a grievance—Dopper hats—A dreary country—In touch with the enemy—An advanced guard affair—Ewart's luck—Blaauwberg—A turning movement—Misjudged distance—The pass gained—A tantalizing situation — Boer tactics — The force against us — Lindley — No telegraph — Boer and British—A bad position—Orders - - - 157-176

CHAPTER IX

LINDLEY TO RHENOSTER RIVER

Leaving Lindley—Two roads—Message to Headquarters—'Gleichen's Horse'—Advanced and rear guards attacked — Rhenoster River—Groot Krantz—Distance from Heilbron—The ox convoy—Message from Spragge—His wants—Our orders—Answer to Spragge—Two unknown facts—Spragge's orders—Two mysteries - - - - - 177-190

CHAPTER X

ROODEPOORT

Roodepoort weakly held—Plan of attack—Surrounded—An artillery duel—Highland Light Infantry pushed forward—A heliograph message—Water in dam—Position at night—Behaviour of troops—Casualties—Strength of enemy—Report to Headquarters—Only a warning—A false guide—Sergeant Bettington—Return of Spragge's messengers - - 191-201

CONTENTS xi

CHAPTER XI

THE LAST MARCH

Order of march—Position of enemy—Country ahead—Plans for the day—An unexpected bombardment—Boer guns silenced—A simple move—A wide extension—Attacks from all sides—Lane to the rescue—Macdonald on ahead—Two men in a buggy—The Landdrost of Heilbron—Startling news—Compensation—Occupation of the town—Up to time—The Highland Brigade—Their Brigadier - - 202-211

CHAPTER XII

HEILBRON

A bad position—Rations—Collecting supplies—A convoy promised—Army across the Vaal—An interview with the inhabitants—No Landdrost—News from Methuen—Escort for convoy—Capture of convoy—Surgeon Connacher's statement—Military precautions—Lovat's Scouts—Their adventures—Food difficulties—The misdirected telegram—Rumours from the railway—Evacuation of sick—A demonstration—Flying columns—Orders from Headquarters—Break up of the Division—Pretoria—Homeward bound—The end of the Division - - - - 212-228

APPENDICES

I. CHIEF STAFF OFFICER'S TIME-TABLE, MARCH 31ST AND APRIL 1ST - - - - 229-233
II. CORRESPONDENCE ON SANNAH'S POST AFFAIR - 234-241
III. EXTRACT FROM ARMY ACT - - - 242

LIST OF MAPS AND PLANS

		PAGE
ACTION AT PAARDEBERG	To face	36
ASSAULT ON CRONJE'S LAAGER	,,	48
ACTION AT POPLAR GROVE	,,	54
COUNTRY TO THE EAST OF BLOEMFONTEIN	,,	72
ROUTE MAP, WINBURG TO HEILBRON	,,	148
ACTION AT BLAAUWBERG	,,	168
ACTION AT ROODEPOORT	,,	192
GENERAL MAP	At end	

THE WORK OF THE NINTH DIVISION

PROLOGUE

THE GUARDS BRIGADE

THE Ninth Division was not born till the 10th February, 1900, but I must touch lightly on the events which preceded its birth, as they had some effect in moulding its destinies.

In the beginning of October, while in command of the Infantry Brigade at Gibraltar, I got my marching orders for South Africa, where I was to command the Guards Brigade, made up of the 3rd Battalion Grenadiers, 1st and 2nd Battalions Coldstream, and 1st Battalion Scots Guards.

On the 12th October I sailed in the freight ship *Ghoorka* with the Grenadiers, taking with me my Brigade-Major, Captain Ruggles-Brise, and my Aide-de-Camp, Captain George Nugent, both Grenadiers.

We landed at Cape Town on the morning of the 15th November; left in the evening by train for

Orange River Station, reaching it in the afternoon of the 17th, and there found Lord Methuen, who commanded our Division. He, like many of us at that time, believed that night attacks would play a great part in the war. There was much to be said for the idea, which I, for one, shared. We believed that the Boers were the better shots, that they would not stand 'cold steel,' and that our discipline was far better than theirs—all points in our favour for night fighting. However, the first thing to be done was to let the troops get their land legs, after three weeks on board ship, and what with settling down, route marching, and one thing and another, we only managed to practise one night march, which was not a great success. The entry in my diary for that evening is: 'Night march, $2\frac{1}{2}$ miles an hour; much too quick, much straggling.'

We left Orange River Station on the 21st, bivouacked next evening at Thomas' Farm, near Belmont, and just before daybreak on the 23rd began our first battle.

Belmont has been called a 'soldiers' fight,' and so it was in the sense that it was won by sheer pluck; but it was a carefully planned one, based on a reconnaissance made by Lord Methuen and the Brigadiers the day before, and an impressionist map issued for their guidance. That the plan then made was not carried out was chiefly due to the fact that we had to make our map as we went, and that there are two sides to every hill, of which we only saw one, while the Boers held the other. Conspicuous, and seemingly standing alone in front of the chain held by the enemy, was a double hill, which Lord Methuen ordered me to take first, giving the main range, to the left, to the Ninth Brigade. In the sketch map issued by the Divisional Staff in the afternoon, this double hill was shown standing alone in the plain, and all orders were based on the belief that it was detached; it was not until the troops reached it in the early dawn of the following morning that it was seen to be joined to another to its right, which it had eclipsed from the point of view whence the reconnaissance was made.

The saddle between the two hills was so slight that they were practically one, and were looked upon as such by the battalion on the right; but this second invisible hill, in its turn, formed part of a piece of ground which the reserve battalions were to occupy, as soon as it had been swept by the fire of the others from the visible one. The result was that the whole force became extended far more to the right than Lord Methuen meant, every battalion but the left one going straight for ground which it was not intended to assault until it had been swept by fire from points already gained.

That was how Belmont became a 'soldiers' battle,' and a very good one, too. The men did for themselves what no General would have dared ask of them, and in four hours had taken a position which, had the scheme been followed, might not have yielded in twelve. The loss was heavy, it is true, but perhaps in a fight lasting all day it might have been as heavy, and, at any rate, I think the moral effect on the men was worth it, for it gave them a knowledge of their own strength which they would not have gained in months of manœuvring.

I shall not try to describe this fight; to do justice to all, it would have to be told in detail from the standpoint of each of the four battalions; but I may say generally that it was divided into three parts: the early morning assault by the Grenadiers and Scots, the later taking of the high hill on the Boers' left by the 1st Coldstream, and the general advance of the whole Brigade.

The leading battalions left their bivouac at two in the morning, and assaulted the hills at the first streak of dawn. By half-past seven it was all over. It was a fight of which all who took part in it had good reason to be proud—regimental officers and men of themselves, and the Generals of their troops; and, unlike most 'soldiers' battles,' it had not the drawback of being due to somebody's mistake, for I do not see that, as far as we were concerned, anything could have been done which would have altered its course. The Staff Officer who made the sketch map on which we worked could only draw what he saw, and if anybody was to blame, it was 'the person or persons unknown' who might have mapped the ground on the other side of the double hill in the days before the Boers came on to it.

Two days later the Division had the fight at Enslin, or Graspan, in which the Guards Brigade was in reserve. We had a good deal of marching, but saw little of the actual work. On the 26th we rested—as much as one does rest in a dust-storm with no tents—and on the 27th made a short march to Kolk Liegte, a farm on the Orange Free State frontier, about three miles to the east of the railway, ten from Jacobsdal, and nine from Modder River Station. I do not remember whether Lord Methuen had said anything to make me think so, but I had an idea that he would take Jacobsdal next, and had chiefly studied one of our very sketchy maps in that direction. We had been told in the afternoon that we should stay where we were the next day, but late at night I was given an order to be ready to march in the morning, and at 4.30 on the 28th I got another to do so at once. I had not taken the 'be ready to march' to mean that the men were to get up at half-past three, and, as they had not had their breakfasts, I told the Staff Officer that I could not start till they had.

We got off at 5.30, and advanced in two columns, the Guards Brigade on the right, and Pole-Carew's Ninth Brigade (which had conformed to our movements) on the left.

At eight o'clock I found Lord Methuen and his Staff looking at a clump of trees some 1,500 yards to our front, which he said was on the Modder River. It had been reported that this was held by the enemy, but he thought they had gone. He, however, ordered me to extend for the attack, swing my right round, and make for a certain tall poplar which he pointed out.

I gave the necessary orders, and the Scots Guards moved off to the right, with their right companies a little thrown forward; the 2nd Coldstream came up on the left, and the Grenadiers in the centre. These last two battalions then halted while the Scots Guards pushed a little more round the flank.

After all our tough work on the kopjes, in which every Boer was behind a stone, ready to slate us as we climbed up painful slopes, it seemed as if we should make short work of the enemy over this nice level ground. We had not been trained to mountain warfare at home, and I think every man felt that, if Boers perched on the top of kopjes were no match for him, they simply had not a chance on the flat. ' Thank God, we've done with those damned kopjes!' or, ' They'll never stand against us here,' was said more than once in my hearing, and these were, I think, fair samples of the general feeling.

As we watched Arthur Paget and his Scots Guards moving ahead to the right, Lord Methuen said to me, ' They are not here.'

' They are sitting uncommonly tight if they are, sir,' I answered; and, as if they had heard him, the Boers answered too with a roar of musketry and a shower of lead which swept away the Scots Guards' machine-gun detachment, and did a good deal of damage generally. I think we were all startled, but everyone was in his place and ready to act; and I remember that before Lord Methuen and I went off to our own business we had time to remark the surprise of his Staff Officers, who had cantered ahead to choose a camping-ground.

When I got to the Scots Guards, I found them with their backs to a river, up the edge of which they had been making their way when the enemy's fire opened. It made a sharp turn to the left a few hundred yards ahead of them, and from the opposite bank of this bend they had been enfiladed. On the further side of this river was a brown grassy plain, stretching towards a low range of hills to the eastward, but bounded to the north, at about half a mile off, by a line of trees, evidently bordering another stream.

The river, running between high banks, was deep, muddy, and at this point unfordable, and my first thought, on finding our way barred by it, was that it was the Modder, for we had always expected to find that deep and wide, but thought the Riet was small. A good look round, however, showed that it must be the Riet, and that the line of trees to the northward marked the course of the Modder. I do not know whether Lord Methuen thought we were further from this river than we were when he told me to swing my right round, or whether he merely thought it was easily fordable; but being where it was, and as deep as it was, it stopped our sweep to the right with the Scots Guards; in fact, they were stopped altogether, for the fire was too hot over the plain to the left to let them advance with their flank to the enemy, while the cross-fire from the bend blocked the way up the river-banks.

As I did not wish to fall back, I sent a message to Codrington, whose 1st Coldstream Battalion was in reserve, to try to find a ford higher up-stream, and hold the further bank. He and Captain Fielding managed to get across themselves, wading chin deep, by choosing a narrow ledge of rocky bottom; but the men who followed them stuck in the mud and were nearly drowned, and on his reporting this I ordered him to give it up.

It is easy enough to be wise after the event, and had I known then what I knew later, I should have run greater risks to get across. The Modder, as we found out next day, was shallow, with a good bottom at a point some hundred yards above its junction with the Riet, and the Boers had no trenches on that part of its banks; therefore if I had got a battalion across between the rivers I should have outflanked the Boers, and stood a good chance of ending the battle early in the day. But, as I have said above, we thought that the Modder would be the harder of the two to cross, and that even if we got to the right bank of the Riet we should be little, if any, better off.

The Ninth Brigade had heard the notes of the much-talked-of pom-pom at Enslin, but until this morning they were unknown to us, and when we heard them for the first time, I think we all agreed that we did not want any more. It is a nasty spiteful-sounding thing; and its string of little shells falling on the dusty ground call to mind the stream from a fire-hose, and seem to have an awkward knack of following one about. I had played hide-and-seek with it on my way to the Scots Guards, and while a small group of us were on the top of the bank trying to make out the lay of the land, the hose was turned on fair into our midst. I have never seen a movement done in better time than the one we then made. Somebody was airing his theories on something or other (in those early days we all had theories), when a cloud of dust jumped up among our feet, and we jumped up too. I do not know what we thought, or whether we thought at all; but two seconds afterwards the same group (theorist and all) was standing, looking rather astonished, at the bottom of the bank. We got used to the pom-pom afterwards, and found its bark a good deal worse than its bite. Of course, men were hit by it from time to time, but the only one I saw in the war was on this afternoon in an old reservoir, in which I had put a Maxim and a couple of companies to sweep the ground between the rivers. It was after the battle had settled into a 'fire fight,' and the men, tired, thirsty, and bored, were dotted about, just waiting for something to happen. I heard a scream and a pom-pom, pom-pom

(I forget which came first), and, turning round, saw the long streak of dust, and a poor fellow in the Scots Guards, who was sitting at the bottom of the bank, fairly in the middle of it. I will not tell what else I saw, but, luckily, he was dead in a few minutes.

The 2nd Coldstream, the Grenadiers, and the left half-battalion of the Scots, tried to advance at first, little by little, and got to within about 800 yards of the Modder; then the fire became too deadly for a thin line, and they had to stop. As long as they lay still little damage was done to them, but quick as thought came a shower of bullets at anyone who rose; and so, as far as we were concerned, the day dragged on till dusk. How Pole-Carew crossed the Modder further down-stream has been told by those who saw it. It is a story worth telling, but not by one who was not there.

The day was a trying one for all, and one that proved the temper of the troops perhaps even more than our slap-dash fight at Belmont. There they were fighting man to man; they had human beings to deal with, and they dealt with them as the British soldier does. But at Modder River there was no human interest—just a bare plain and, 800 yards off, a line of trees; not a Boer, or even a puff of smoke, to be seen all day; only, if one raised his head, the ping of a bullet and the sight of another dead or wounded comrade.

Although this had not been intended at first,

THE GUARDS BRIGADE

Pole-Carew's turning movement made the Guards Brigade a 'containing force,' and as such we were doing good work; but the men, of course, did not know this, and to them the purpose of those weary hours under a dropping fire must have been a mystery. For ten hours they lay, hungry and thirsty, in the scorching sun, with nothing but that line of trees to aim at, knowing nothing of what was happening in other parts of the field, but only sure of one thing—that there they must stay till the order came to move.

A force treble our strength, losing heavily, could have rushed the river; if we had gone to work some other way, perhaps we should have slept at Modder River Station that night, perhaps we should not; but all that I am trying to do is to say what did happen —to the Guards Brigade.

At about 5.30 in the afternoon my orderly said he had heard that Lord Methuen was wounded, and an hour later came a note from the Divisional Signalling Officer saying Lord Methuen wished me to put Major Benson in the place of Colonel Northcote, his D.A.A.G., who had been killed. As this was purely a divisional matter, it seemed to confirm the report, so I handed over the Brigade to Paget, and took command of the Division. I had intended to try a rush soon after sunset, hoping that in the semi-dusk the Boers' fire would be wild enough to let us reach the Modder banks, and told this to Paget when I handed the Brigade to him; but he was strongly against it, with fagged, hungry men, and I am glad that I took his advice not to try it. If I had known as much then as I did afterwards, I should not have thought of it. Perhaps the Boers were weak in 'fire discipline' and wasteful of ammunition, and, according to the book, should not have done what they did in the dark; but after Magersfontein we learnt that something thicker than darkness was wanted to keep the bullets off.

I had hoped to get away before dusk, to see what was going on on the left; but Paget was with his battalion when I heard of Lord Methuen's wound, and some time was spent in getting at him, making plans for the morrow, and settling how to feed the men for the night, so that it was past sunset before I got off, and pitch dark before I hit the railway, on the further side of which was the Ninth Brigade. Shots still dropped in now and then from the Boer trenches, but all heavy firing had ceased, so I made a ganger's hut on the line my Headquarters, and sent Nugent to look for some of the Divisional Staff. He stumbled about among the waggons and barked his shins, and came back after about an hour empty-handed, but full of wrath at someone who led him a mile down the line the wrong way. However, I got hold of a Staff Officer at last, and issued orders for the next morning. These were to hold the old reservoir with one battalion, and reinforce Pole-Carew with the rest.

This was done, and, as the Boers had been firing

after sunset, we could only act on the belief that they were still about, and had to set to work prepared for a fight. It was reported once that the enemy held the east of the village, but this proved to be false, and at about eleven we settled down round Modder River Station without having fired a shot.

In the meanwhile Lord Methuen had sent for me, and said that he felt well enough to take over the Division again, so I returned to the Brigade.

On the afternoon of December 10th, Brigadiers were ordered to meet Lord Methuen about four miles out on the Kimberley road. We found him, with his leg still bandaged, sitting on the box-seat of a waggon, on a ridge facing Magersfontein Kopje, which from the same ridge our artillery was pounding. The Highland Brigade was bivouacked in the valley below, and to the right.

Methuen said he was going to attack with the Highland Brigade before dawn, and that the Guards were to march in the night, so as to come up just before daylight. As we had had our share up to Modder River, and the Highlanders were fresh, we were to be in reserve.

We marched at one in a thunderstorm, and about as inky a night as I ever remember—one of those nights in which one literally cannot see one's hand; but we got there in time, and halted in the place where the Highlanders had been. With the first streak of dawn, when one could just see a man a couple of feet off, came a roar of musketry. That first fusillade at Modder River had been fairly thick, but it was nothing to this; from its volume I thought that both sides must be firing as hard as they could, as it did not seem likely that only one could be making so much noise, and, remembering Belmont, fancied that when day broke we should see the kilts on the kopje-tops.

I had had a few minutes' talk with Wauchope the afternoon before, and had said to him that, as we were in reserve, I did not suppose we should see much of the fight. He shook his head, and said:

Things do not always go as they are expected; you may not be in reserve for long.' I thought of this then, but, picturing the Highlanders already halfway up the kopje, felt that we were out of it for this day.

Daylight grows quickly in South Africa, and we were not left in doubt for many minutes. We could see little from where we were, but as the day dawned Methuen could make out that the Highlanders had been repulsed, and sent us an order to push on to a ridge to our right front and hold it with our three battalions, he keeping the Scots as Divisional troops. Later I had an order to support the Highlanders, and got together all the men I could to do so; but by this time we were held in front, our right was hard pressed, and, with some three miles of front to cover with only three battalions, I could not spare more than two companies from the firing line; to these, however, I added half my reserve. Later in the day the Scots Guards were given us to prolong our left.

Magersfontein was an eventful and heavy day for the Highlanders, but only a trying one for us. We were ordered not to advance, and had nothing much to look forward to, so we simply lay in the sun till our clothes were dry, and when it got hot wished they were wet again. We were under fire all day, but it was never as heavy as at Modder River, and there was also more cover.

At last night fell, and a very cold night it was for hungry, tired men. Although we had been on our legs nearly all the night before, most of us found doing 'sentry go' in front of our bivouac more comfortable than lying still and shivering.

At dawn I went to the Divisional Headquarters, and on hearing from Methuen that he intended to retire at once, said that I thought that we could well hold on, and that if we did the Boers would go. So he gave me leave to choose sites for some half-battalion works which I proposed, and sent his Chief Engineer round with me to carry out my plans. An hour later, however, he changed his mind, and called a council of war, in which I was outvoted, so it was settled that the force should retire at noon, and that I was to command the rear-guard. This was made up of the Guards and Cavalry Brigades, the latter with its Horse Artillery and a battery of Field Artillery.

We were then holding the ridge we had held all the day before, to the right front of the kopje, which our left slightly overlapped. The enemy held the trenches at the foot of the kopje, and their extension, about 800 yards in front of us, which reached to the river. I gave orders that the artillery were to retire first, and take up a position on the ridge about a mile back, which had been Divisional Headquarters. As soon as they had gained this, the Scots and two Coldstream battalions were to begin their retirement, the Grenadiers holding on to the advanced ridge till the others were abreast of Headquarter Hill.

My Staff thought the enemy would advance as soon as the retirement began, and that the Grenadiers would find themselves hard pressed, but I did not agree with them.

As soon as our artillery began to move, that of the enemy opened fire, and threw up a good deal of dust round our guns and waggons. There are few pleasanter sights for an Englishman than that of our artillery moving under fire. Nearly everybody gets cool when 'the guns begin to shoot,' but I know of nothing which conveys by its manner such an utter disregard for the enemy's efforts as a British battery quietly trotting along under a heavy shower of shells.

Shortly afterwards the Grenadiers got the same chance, of which they took the fullest advantage. I had often thought at home that we did not practise rear-guard actions quite enough, but if Crabbe and his men had been doing nothing else all their lives they could not have carried it out more neatly. As soon as they began to move, the enemy's guns turned most of their attention to them, and at times Crabbe's lines could hardly be seen through the dust; but when we did see them they were strolling quietly along in slow time, utterly unconcerned, alternate files halting and facing the enemy, while the others retired to a fresh position, in which they halted till the advanced files had passed through them. In Hyde Park the movement would have been called perfect; at Aldershot it would have been said that it was too regular and slow; at Magersfontein it, at all events, showed the Boers that, if the British soldier does not mean to hurry, it is not easy to make him do so. One of them had said of George Nugent at the Modder River fight: 'He rides about on his —— old white horse, and don't care a ——, and just says, "Let the —— shoot."' Whether my Aide-de-Camp was correctly reported I do not know—perhaps he looked it more than said it; and every man of the Grenadiers looked it so thoroughly as they sauntered across that mile of shell-swept plain, that, thinking of the story, I could almost hear a murmur from the ranks of, 'Let the —— shoot.'

Soon after the Grenadiers got abreast of Headquarter Hill the Boer fire ceased, and we marched back to camp without hearing another shot.

I will not describe the next dreary six weeks: how we trenched and demonstrated, how we had scares and slept in our boots, and read the telegrams from Natal and did not understand them.

CHAPTER I

THE PAARDEBERG MARCH

ON the 10th February I was sent for to Headquarters, and told that I was to have command of the newly-formed Ninth Division, made up of Macdonald's Highland Brigade (Black Watch, Argyll and Sutherland, Seaforths, and Highland Light Infantry) and Smith Dorrien's Nineteenth Brigade (Shropshires, Gordons, Duke of Cornwall's Light Infantry, and the Canadians). I was to march next morning, but should get further orders. In the meanwhile my Staff had to be chosen and got together.

A Divisional Staff consists of a Chief Staff Officer (Assistant-Adjutant-General), three Deputy-Assistant - Adjutant - Generals, an Assistant - Provost-Marshal, a Divisional Signalling Officer, a Principal Medical Officer and his Secretary, a Commanding Royal Engineer, a Chaplain, a Transport Officer, and two Aides-de-Camp.

My Aide-de-Camp, George Nugent, followed me as a matter of course, and I asked for my Brigade-Major Ruggles-Brise as my Deputy - Assistant-Adjutant-General. Macdonald recommended his Brigade-Major, Lieutenant-Colonel Ewart, as Chief

THE PAARDEBERG MARCH

Staff officer, and this was agreed to; he in his turn recommended Browne of the Highland Light Infantry, Campbell of the Cameron Highlanders, and Aston of the Marines, as Signalling Officer, Second Aide-de-Camp, and Provost-Marshal. The rest were chosen by Headquarters, making the list, not yet quite complete, as follows:

- A.A.G.: Lieutenant-Colonel E. S. Ewart, Cameron Highlanders.
- D.A.A.G. (*a*): Captain H. Ruggles-Brise, Grenadier Guards.
- D.A.A.G. (*b*): Captain H. L. Humphreys,* Army Service Corps.
- D.A.A.G. (Intelligence): Major A. E. W. Count Gleichen, C.M.G.,† Grenadier Guards.
- C.R.E.: Colonel J. C. Barker, Royal Engineers.
- P.M.O.: Lieutenant-Colonel J. C. Dorman, M.B., R.A.M.C.*
- P.M.O.'s Secretary: Major R. Bond, R.A.M.C.†
- Transport Officer: Major S. S. Long,† Army Service Corps.
- Signalling Officer: Lieutenant A. N. E. Browne, Highland Light Infantry.
- Assistant-Provost-Marshal: Lieutenant H. E. Raymond,‡ Yorkshire Regiment.
- Chaplain (Presbyterian): Rev. J. Robertson.
- Aides-de-Camp: Captain G. Nugent, Grenadier Guards; Lieutenant Hon. R. Campbell,‡ Cameron Highlanders.

* Joined at Gras Pan.   † Joined at Paardeberg.
‡ Joined at Bloemfontein.

Of these, Ewart, Barker, Ruggles-Brise, Browne, and Nugent were on the spot, and the rest were to join me as they could.

Probably a Staff has rarely been got together in a much greater hurry, and, I am sure, never has a better one been formed. I do not say this from any feeling that a General ought to do so, but simply because from first to last every one of them did that which it was his business to do as well as it could possibly be done. We were all human beings, and we all made mistakes, though I do not think we made many. Most of us had been in queer climates, and we were not always at our best; but for good solid hard work and all-round common-sense I have not yet come across any dozen men who could beat those who helped me for the next few months.

In the afternoon I saw Lord Roberts and got my orders, which were to concentrate at Ramdam on the 13th, and thence march viâ Waterval Drift to Jacobsdal, which I was to occupy without fighting if possible, but, if it resisted, after bombardment.

The Highlanders were at Modder River, and it was arranged that they were to go by train to Enslin, and thence act as escort to an ammunition column, while I went on to Gras Pan to meet the newly-formed Nineteenth Brigade.

We made an early start, but did not get to Gras Pan till about three in the afternoon, and there found Smith-Dorrien waiting for his Brigade to grow; this it did bit by bit as trains came in, and by midnight it and my Staff were fairly complete.

Things did not look very hopeful as we marched off in the early dawn next morning. Our transport had all come from the South, and dropped in during the evening and night, so that, except by lantern light, I had never seen the animals which were to drag our waggons across the Free State. It was not long, however, before I learnt something of them and their many failings. I have no wish to say anything against them as mules : when they left their native heaths or pampas, or wherever they came from, I dare say they were as good as their fellows ; but a long sea-voyage, instantly followed by a long railway journey, is not the best training for a long trek, and the fittest of them would not have been really up to the mark with less than a month's rest, while 'as to' the worst, as one of the correspondents said of a distinguished General, 'Oh, Lord !' Veterinary officers could not afford to be very particular in those days, but they had had to cast 370 of them as unfit for work, and, fit or unfit, the poor brutes had to do it as best they could.

We had not been many minutes on the march before it was reported to me that one of the Gordons' waggons had broken down, then one of the Canadians'; and so it went on till it was obvious that we could not get on with the loads we were carrying. The end of it was that I had to order a large percentage of the greatcoats to be left behind.

I believe a greatcoat had been weighed at Headquarters, and that this weight, multiplied by a certain figure, had been taken to represent a proper waggon-load. I would sooner speak disrespectfully of the Equator than throw any doubt on the weights and measures of the Headquarter Staff; but greatcoats, even under like conditions, are by no means all of the same weight, and but a slight knowledge of physics is enough to teach us that cloth saturated with water weighs more than the same stuff when its pores are filled with air. So that although a waggon full of dry greatcoats, all equal to the sample, might be a fair load for a fair team, the same coats when damp would make a very unfair load; and if the question is further complicated by a team of only about half the regulation pulling-power, it will be understood that something had to be left behind, and why a good many of my men had to shiver through the nights for a long time to come. Perhaps it may be asked why I did not leave something else; but we had no tents, and ammunition and food are even more necessary than coats. It is true I might have made the men carry their coats while their blankets were carried for them, which would, perhaps, have got us over the first day's march. But a regulation greatcoat is not a nice thing to go into battle with; it stands out very black against the khaki, and when the men lie down the rolls on their backs show up like so many 'bull's eyes' for the enemy to aim at. Also the coat is not so generally useful as the blanket, which is a covering (not thick enough) by night, and, with a couple of sticks, makes a shelter from the sun by day.

The men got on well enough—at least, those who were allowed to do so; for I had to keep a good many back to help along the lengthening string of waggons, and, although the head of the Division halted for the day by noon, it was past sunset before the rearguard marched into Ramdam. Here I found the Highland Brigade, Colonel Cholmondeley's City Imperial Volunteers, and Grant's Naval guns. Odds and ends of the Staff dropped in during the day, and before night the Ninth Division could be fairly counted as formed. Ramdam was a typical Free State homestead, and when I have described it I have, with slight differences, described them all. Of course, there was the dam or glorified horse-pond, without which no Free State farm could exist. In calling it a dam, cause and effect are rather mixed, but that is the name by which it is always known. The Free State is mostly a land of ridges and furrows, and, having selected the particular ridge on which he wishes to build his farm, the Free Stater proceeds to make a dam across the vale below. Sometimes there is only a bog, sometimes it is fed by a streamlet, running after rain, and dry in summer; but in any case the rains are enough to fill the hollow, and provide dirty water through the drought for himself, and his ox, and his ass, and the stranger within his gates.

I have drunk so much dirty water in my life with so little ill effect that it is not a thing I am very particular about; but my Staff (with the P.M.O. to instruct them) knew all about bacilli and such-like, and filtered the water during the few days that the filters lasted, and boiled it up to the end. As 25 per cent. of them got enteric fever, it seems likely that water is not the only source of that disease, and I am inclined to think that more of it is carried in the dust than in anything else. But to return to our homestead: On the edge of the pond are a few willows, and on the ridge facing the water a square whitewashed house with corrugated iron roof, and round it some outhouses and cattle-kraals.

Kelly-Kenny's Division had passed through before us, and with him were Rimington's Guides, which was patent even without their title in letters of chalk over the doorway; for the 'Tigers,' though unequalled alike for fighting and scouting, are not men whom I should invite to bivouac on my estate.

The entrance, which had been closed by double doors, led into a square whitewashed hall and dining-room, whence opened four smaller rooms, strewn in picturesque confusion with such articles as are of no use in a campaign. Opposite the front-door was that of the kitchen, and behind that, on the other side of the yard, the Kaffir quarters.

We were off next morning at half-past four, and,

marching by a fairly good road, struck the Riet River at Waterval Drift by noon. Here we found the Headquarter Staff in occupation of the farmhouse on the left bank, and got orders to march at one next morning, as Lord Roberts said the men would fall out less by marching in the cool hours. This was an experiment which we were trying backwards and forwards throughout the campaign; and there is a good deal to be said on both sides. Perhaps with a full moon, as we had then, the night march is worth doing, but even at the best of times it takes longer than a day one, and I think on the whole wears out the men more. For a force which has tents in which the men can sleep by day, it may pay, but it is not very easy to sleep in the sun; and after a good many trials my Brigadiers and I found that we got the best results by starting at the first streak of dawn, and then marching about fifteen miles. If the whole march was much over that, we halted for a meal; if not, marched straight on to our bivouac. When in touch with the enemy this plan had to be somewhat altered to suit the animals, as oxen will not eat at night, and therefore do better if night marches are made, while horses and mules require a halt for water early in the day. With a large force of cavalry to protect the transport this can easily be managed at all times, and when there was no chance of fighting the oxen were sent ahead at night, and the mule transport left behind at the morning halt; but sometimes, as we found ourselves later, with a large mixed convoy, practically no mounted troops, and continually harassed by the enemy, it was no easy matter to suit all tastes.

The Riet River runs between high, sandy banks, and we found the drift a very difficult one. In spite of his thirty-six oxen a gun, and 400 men turned on to the pull-ropes, Grant had his work cut out to get his Four Point Sevens up the further slope, and we had to keep permanent fatigue parties of 200 men at work till midnight, helping the transport across. People who have not tried it have no idea of the amount of work and organization a bad drift brings on the Staff, though I must say, for mine, that the more they got the more they seemed to want. It was in vain that I preached to Ewart and Ruggles-Brise, that if they kept on as they were going they would both be in hospital before long; but nothing would make them rest, and I suppose they knew their own constitutions best, as my forebodings were never realized.

In the afternoon we got an order from Headquarters to leave the ox transport behind under a 'suitable escort,' as Lord Roberts did not wish it to march by day. Ewart, who received the order, and who is a man of great and varied Staff experience, insisted on being told what sized escort was considered suitable, and got an order that 200 men were enough. After we left they were attacked in force, and all the waggons captured. Our escort made a most gallant defence, but as I did not see it I shall not attempt to describe it.

A ten-miles march over a stony and barren country brought us to Wegdrai Drift, where we found the Seventh Division, one of the Brigades of which, however, had to go back to Waterval to rescue the escort for the convoy, and when we marched next morning for Jacobsdal the Highlanders were left behind to take its place.

Jacobsdal had been occupied the day before without any heavy fighting, and after only a five-miles march we thought we were going to have an easy day of it; but we had barely settled down in our bivouac when Lord Roberts sent for me to say there was a report that the enemy was advancing from the south, and that the Nineteenth Brigade must stand to its arms till further orders. Soon afterwards he sent for me again, and gave me orders to start for Kimberley that evening with the whole division. This was after French's relief of it, so there was no great chance of fighting; but water was reported to be scarce after crossing the Modder, and a good many arrangements had to be made. By six in the evening I had got everything cut and dried, and had learnt all I could about the road from the guides, when a Staff Officer handed me an order to march to Klip Drift on the Modder instead. As we were to take a good deal more transport with us by this route than by the other, fresh arrangements had to be made, and it was half-past nine o'clock before the Transport Officer reported that he was ready.

In the afternoon an order had come out saying that in consequence of the prevalence of looting Lord Roberts had determined to take stringent measures to stop it. My Staff were just discussing this, and wondering who would be the first victims, when Sergeant Gale, our energetic Provost-Sergeant, appeared, followed by one of my orderlies, whom he said he had just caught 'commandeering' a watch. This distinctly came under the head of a 'regrettable incident.' The orderly was a capital fellow, and the watch seemed a very poor one to hang a man for; but discipline had to be kept up, and I could only tell Sergeant Gale to do his duty, which was to march the prisoner to the Provost-Marshal at Headquarters. I wasted so much pity on the offender during the night march that I felt almost injured when, as dawn broke next morning, I saw him in his usual place near me, and asked him, perhaps rather unsympathetically, how on earth he got there. He said that the Provost-Marshal had ordered him to return to his duty, and, as Sergeant Gale confirmed this, I was glad to welcome the lost sheep. As during the next few weeks we were too busy being shot at to have any time for hanging each other, the matter dropped; but I tell the story to show that human weaknesses found their way even into the Ninth Division.

We marched at ten that evening, and all went

smoothly till, at about two, a sharp ''Alt! who goes there?' rang out of the gloom a few yards to our front.

'Friend,' answered Ewart, who was riding at my side.

'Advance one, and give the countersign,' said the voice.

'Kimberley' (or whatever it was), said Ewart.

'No, that ain't it,' said the voice.

So Ewart cantered forward, and a lengthy conversation took place, in which such scraps as 'damned nonsense' and 'them's my orders' seemed to crop up a good deal. It was a ridiculous situation—a whole Brigade hurrying to the front stopped by one stupid little sentry; but he evidently meant to stand up for his rights, and if we had tried to play the 'brutal majority' trick on him would probably have opened magazine fire, and perhaps done some damage. So, seeing that the only course was to try kindness, I, too, rode forward, and did my best to explain that our countersign was the genuine article freshly made at Headquarters; but he had heard too much about Boer 'slimness' to be taken in with cock-and-bull stories like that, and neither gentleness nor threats would move him from his resolve to defend the drift (his post was at the edge of a dry watercourse) with the last drop of his blood. At last we extracted from him that his piquet was about a mile to the south-eastward, and got a very unwilling consent that an officer should ride forward to refer the matter to its commander. This proved to be a Mounted Infantry subaltern, who had been posted there (he said) a week ago, and thought he had been forgotten; he knew nothing of the enemy, or French, or Kelly-Kenny, or, indeed, of anything that we wanted to know, and after about three-quarters of an hour's delay we left him, more in sorrow than in anger, to his rather vague duty.

Half an hour afterwards came another 'Halt! who goes there?' and refusal to accept our countersign; but there are limits to patience, and it was Smith-Dorrien this time who acted as forerunner. I did not catch exactly what he said to that sentry, but from the little I heard I am sure that I could not print it here, and soon afterwards Smith-Dorrien reappeared out of the darkness with a cowed and apologetic young officer, who said Kelly-Kenny's Division was about a mile ahead. In this he deceived us, but it cheered us up, and I have no doubt he meant it kindly.

At four we passed a farmhouse, and I was looking back to see if I had got too far ahead of the troops, when, catching a little glimmer in the window, I sent Nugent back to find out what it was, and learnt that it came from a telegraph-station, and that Kitchener was encamped close by. After some stumbling about I found him, having finished his breakfast and ready to start. He said that Kelly-Kenny had just marched off, and he seemed to have expected us sooner, so I explained the changes of order of the day before, and how up till the last minute we had been preparing for the march to Kimberley. He seemed very much surprised at this, and, after saying that we were to follow on to Koedoesrand Drift in the afternoon, rode off to join Kelly-Kenny.

Kelly-Kenny had been fighting near this place the day before, and when day broke we found that the farmhouse was full of his wounded, of whom a good many more had not yet been brought in.

The Highland Brigade had marched by the direct road from Wegdrai to Klip Kraal, about four miles up-stream, so I sent a message to Macdonald, telling him when I intended to march, and that he was to keep ahead of us.

We got off again at about half-past four in the afternoon, but on coming abreast of Klip Kraal were delayed by some Mounted Infantry transport crossing our front, and by the time they were clear it was dark. The moon that day rose at about eight, and I had intended to halt for the men's evening meal during the hour and a half of darkness, and then push on; but there were so many waggons on the road going the same way that Smith-Dorrien begged me to give them a good start, in order that when we did march we might be clear of the dust and not be delayed; so I settled to halt till ten.

I do not think many of us had got much sleep at

Klip Drift; we had been on our legs all the day and night before, and were getting rather fagged. I do not know what others thought of it, but it seemed an uncommonly long night to me, and I was never more pleased to hear the accent of the North than when an unmistakably Scotch challenge told us that we had overtaken the Highland Brigade.

Having found Macdonald, I learnt that he had marched straight on, and got there between one and two; he believed Kelly-Kenny and Kitchener were somewhere near, but had heard no news.

Finding a deserted farmhouse close by, I tumbled on to a singularly dirty mattress, and Smith-Dorrien's Brigade having halted in rear of the Highlanders, every man except the unlucky sentries was soon fast asleep.

CHAPTER II

PAARDEBERG

AT five on the morning of the 18th February I was roused by Ewart, who said the enemy was advancing from the east. From our bivouac, which was near the Modder, nothing was to be seen but the kopje known as Paardeberg, on the north bank of the river, and a stony ridge running round the skyline on our side. So I jumped on my horse and galloped off to a point on this ridge, from which I thought I should get the best view, sending for Lieutenant-Colonel Tylden, who commanded my Howitzer Battery.

From a spur in the ridge running towards the river, to which I made my way, I could see the Modder winding from the eastwards for about a mile, and then making a sharp bend to the south. On the rising ground to our south-east were British troops, which I assumed to be of Kelly-Kenny's Division. In the scrub by the river-banks under us to the north-east were a few of Martyr's Mounted Infantry exchanging shots with the Boers; and about two and a half miles to the eastward, on the further bank of the river, was the Boer laager.

As Kelly-Kenny was holding all the ground to our right, and as I knew French's Cavalry were due from Kimberley with orders to make for Koedoesrand, it seemed to me that we could be of little use on the south bank, so told Ewart that I should leave half a battalion and some guns to hold the gap between Kelly-Kenny's left and the river, and take the rest of the division across to close round Cronje from the north-west.

He was just writing orders to this effect, when Martyr reported that, owing to a sudden flood, some of his men who were on the north bank were unable to get back, and that the river was quite impassable for infantry. Our pontoons had been left at Klip Drift by order of the Chief of the Staff, as their waggons were wanted for transport purposes; but we had one section of a James' Collapsible Boat, so I told Colonel Barker, my Commanding Royal Engineer, to get a rope across with this and to do his best to improve the drift. He suggested running some waggons into the river to break the force of the stream.

As the troops had not had their breakfast, this seemed a good chance for them to do so; I therefore sent for half a battalion of the Highlanders as escort for the 65th and 82nd Batteries, which I had ordered up, and told the rest to stand fast. Soon after six, however, I saw that the enemy in the scrub below us were too strong for the Mounted Infantry to deal with, and seemed inclined to advance under cover of the banks, so told Macdonald to bring up the rest of his brigade and clear this ground before we crossed.

Just as he was beginning this movement, Hamilton, Kitchener's D.A.A.G., brought a verbal message* that I was to reinforce Kelly-Kenny with my whole Division, including the Howitzer and Field Batteries. I sent him the batteries as ordered, and told him he should have Macdonald as soon as the scrub was cleared, and Smith-Dorrien as soon as he could be ready.

About a quarter of an hour after the batteries had advanced, I noticed that the Boers were moving in force along the river-bed where it makes the big bend to the south, and into a patch of scrub running to the northward from this bend, and it seemed certain that if we did not stop them they would either be able to escape that way or outflank us. So, failing any infantry till the drift was passable, I thought the best thing to do was to make their advance as unpleasant as possible with artillery, and sent a message to the 82nd Battery to come back at once. It made very good practice; but the Boers had got cover before we could open fire, and we were unable to turn them out that day.

Kitchener seems also to have seen this move-

* I took these orders from the Chief of the Staff, as representing Lord Roberts; but, as Kelly-Kenny was the senior General present, I suppose they came theoretically from him.

ment, for an hour later I received an order from him to push Smith-Dorrien's Brigade and the 82nd Battery across the river, and, thanks to the hard work of the 7th Company Royal Engineers, under Kincaid, the passage was begun at nine. The water was shoulder-deep and the current strong, but all got safely over, and the machine guns were taken in the section of the James' Boat. By a quarter past ten all were across and the turning movement well developed. Smith-Dorrien sent the Canadians to work up the river bank, their right forming the pivot of the movement, and their left joining the right of the Shropshires, whose left in turn touched the right of the Gordons. The latter were accompanied by the 82nd Battery, and their objective was a knoll commanding the scrub at the river's bend, which I have noticed before.

This knoll—Gun Hill, as we called it—was occupied by the Shropshires soon after eleven, the Gordons still swinging round to prolong the line to the left, and by four o'clock Smith-Dorrien was well round two sides of the scrub.

In the meanwhile the Highlanders had advanced to join Kelly-Kenny, marching in file, in single rank, with about four paces between each man, at a fairly safe distance from the river. I watched them moving across the plain, and, after wondering a little what they could be wanted for, turned my glasses on to the more easily-understood movements of Smith-Dorrien, till one of my Staff pointed

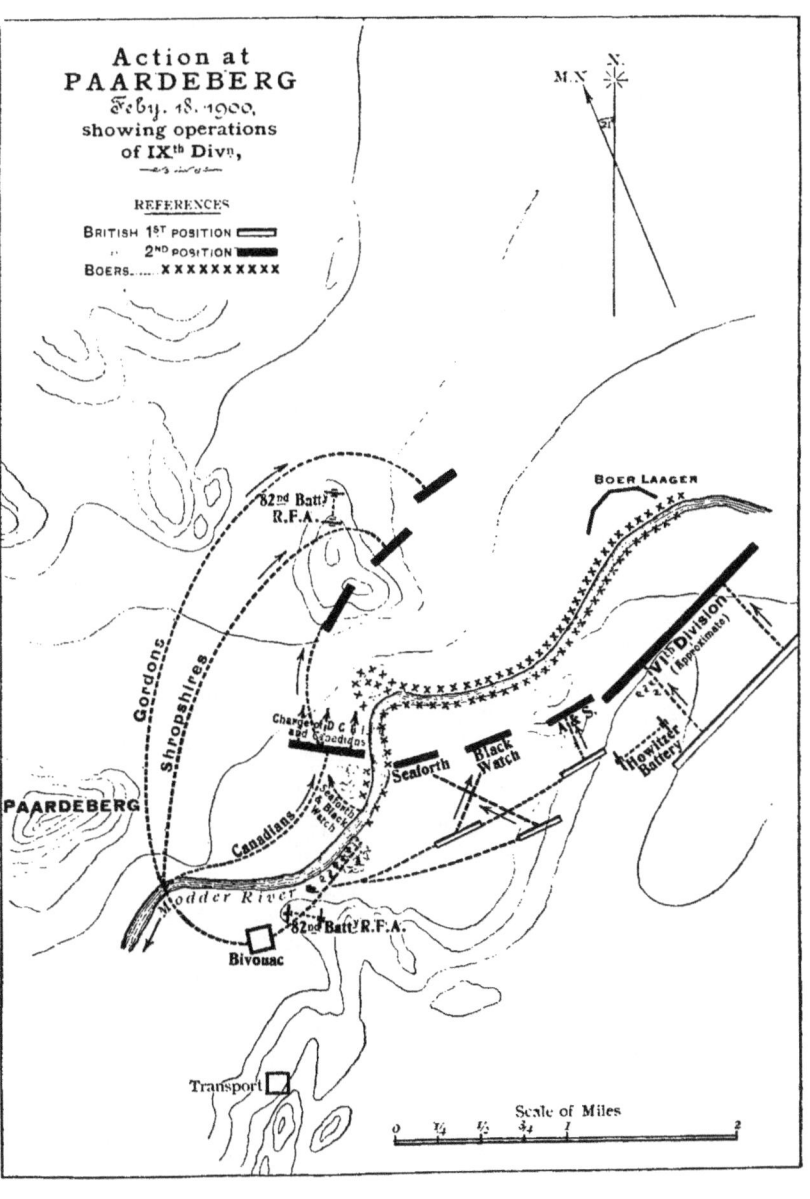

out that the Highlanders had turned to their front and were advancing straight at the river. In any case I should not have called them back; a movement of this sort, once launched, must be allowed to take its course. And, apart from its bad moral effect, a retirement across that plain would have cost as many lives as an advance. But as it was, they were out of my hands; they had been ordered to reinforce Kelly-Kenny, and their right was actually overlapping his left when they advanced; and I could only suppose that the movement had been ordered by him or the Chief of the Staff. Whether it was so or not, I do not know to this day; but whoever ordered it, it was a very fine feat on the part of the Highlanders, and one of which they will always have reason to be proud. One can hardly say the ground was worse for advancing over under fire than that which the Guards had to deal with at the Modder River fight, for that would be impossible to find; but it was certainly as bad, and I never hope to see or read of anything grander than the advance of that thin line across the coverless plain, under a hail of lead from their invisible enemy in the river-banks.

Thinner and thinner it grew, and thicker and thicker the brown patches on the grass behind it. What men are able to do, the Highlanders did; but there seems to be some law which fixes the exact amount of thinning which a body of civilized men can stand. It has nothing to do with fear: a battalion will advance without a waver, under a storm of bullets, up to a certain point; on reaching that point it is possible that the enemy's fire may have slackened, but if the gaps in the ranks are too big it will halt.

I am not going to argue on the vexed question of extended *versus* close formation for attack, but there are two things quite certain: First, that frontal attacks against entrenched troops with modern rifles cannot be pushed home as a single extended line; and, second, that one cannot advance in close order unless one has got the men.

Had the two and a half divisions at Paardeberg advanced on the front covered by the Highland Brigade, they would probably have got home, but then Cronje would not have been surrounded, and, unless one prevents him doing so, a Boer who does not want to fight takes the obvious course of walking away.

The critical point which I have spoken of above had been reached by Kelly-Kenny's left battalion at about 800 yards from the river, and into this the Argyll and Sutherland Highlanders merged and halted. The Black Watch and Seaforths marched on for another 300 yards, but the advance of the Canadians having cleared the north bank for some distance, the Seaforths found themselves overlapping the enemy's right, and Urmston, who was commanding them, managed to get two and a half of his companies up to, and over, the river. They advanced along this to within 200 yards of the Boer trenches, accompanied by another Seaforth company and two of the Black Watch which had crossed lower down.

Macdonald, who had been with his Brigade throughout this advance, then retired to a ridge occupied by the Howitzer Battery, about a mile and a half to the eastward, from which he could get a good view of the ground covered by his Brigade. While there he was wounded in the ankle by a chance bullet—a curious piece of bad luck. He was succeeded in command by Colonel Hughes-Hallett, but took his place again, still rather lame, before we reached Bloemfontein.

As far as my Division was concerned, the fighting was now all round the clump of scrub in the bend; rushes were made at it from time to time, but without result, and it was so nearly surrounded by our infantry that the gunners did not like to give it the pounding that it required.

At about one o'clock Kitchener came to me and asked if I had got any fresh troops to spare for a more determined assault. I told him my only reserve was half the Duke of Cornwall's Light Infantry, guarding the Transport, and he said this half battalion must cross over and rush the position. He asked Ewart to lead them across, and told him what he wished done. I therefore sent for Colonel Aldworth, commanding the battalion, and told him the Chief of the Staff's wishes, and, on hearing from him that his men were about to have their dinners, put off the advance till they had done; for it did not strike me as a task to be undertaken on an empty stomach.

Guided by Ewart, they started at about half-past three, and crossed the river at the point where the Seaforths had done so in the morning, and then extended to the left. They were joined by the Canadians and the four Seaforth companies, and, creeping steadily on till within 500 yards of the enemy, charged forward with a ringing cheer. 'By Jove, they've done it!' somebody said at my side. And I own I, too, thought they had; it seemed as if nothing could stop them.

But the fatal moment came for them as it had come for others, and when within 200 yards of the enemy, those that were left had to halt. Aldworth, gallantly leading them, was killed, and the casualties in his half-battalion were over 22 per cent. The Canadians also suffered heavily—their percentage of casualties that day was double that of either of the other two battalions; but I do not know how many of them were due to this charge. The Seaforth casualty list was also about 25 per cent. in excess of that of the Black Watch or Argyll and Sutherland, but I am also uncertain as to exactly how it was raised.

This effort practically ended our work for the day. As dusk set in, the right of the Highlanders was withdrawn to form a chain of outposts on the ridge to the south, and part of Smith-Dorrien's Brigade was moved on to higher ground to the north; otherwise the troops bivouacked where they were, some of them over a mile from the nearest water, all tired and hungry, and many of them wet; but if the consciousness of having done one's duty is any help to sleep under adverse conditions, they should have slept well.

A very able Staff Officer said to me when talking about another fight, 'The worst of war is that one cannot try things both ways.' Perhaps if Paardeberg had to be fought again to-morrow, it would be worked differently on both sides, and maybe it would end differently; but I, for one, cannot tell what that end would be till I have seen the trial. It seems, therefore, the wisest plan to take it as it stands, and also to take it for granted that everyone did what he thought best at the time. But although I do not see much sense in dwelling on what might have been, but was not, I think what was—be it good or bad—is all the better told, and therefore I have written of what I saw. For once I am sorry that it is beyond the scope of this book to write also of what others saw, for the things that brave men did that day and never talked about afterwards should not be hidden.

When the next day broke, Smith-Dorrien found that hateful clump of scrub by the bend was at last empty, and that the river-banks were clear for about 1,500 yards above it; so he pushed his left forward and threw up a shelter trench. The ground which the Highlanders' right had held was still under Boer fire, and many of the dead had to lie where they were. Daylight also showed that Kelly-Kenny's and my Divisions were a good deal overlapped, and the morning was spent in shaking down into our proper places.

About noon Lord Roberts rode up, having come straight through from Jacobsdal, and shortly afterwards firing ceased, and we heard that Cronje had offered to surrender. I know nothing of the inner workings of all this, but in the afternoon our guns opened fire again.

The next week was mostly spent in digging and bombarding, the spade work being done chiefly on the right bank, and that of the guns on the left. Oddly enough, we had got nearly as many guns as spades; but in this case I am inclined to think the humbler and rather despised engine of war was the more useful of the two.

The Boer is a very practical sort of man, and, although he can be as brave as anybody else if he thinks it worth while, does not seem to get any pleasure out of being shot at, and generally thinks out for himself the best way of avoiding that condition at the moment. Finding himself in a tight corner, therefore, his first idea was to put his body in a safe place, and his second to make that place as poor a target for our guns as possible. These ideas he carried into effect by digging a bottle-shaped trench, just wide enough at the top to let his body through, and undercut enough to give shelter even from vertical fire. The earth thrown out was scattered broadcast, and in the absence of the nice little parapet which we put up, it was hardly possible, even from the balloon, to see exactly where the trenches were, and less so to hit anyone inside them. The result was that, though our shells set fire to many of the waggons and killed most of the horses and cattle, so at once crippling the Boers' mobility and lessening their food-supply, they did little harm to the men.

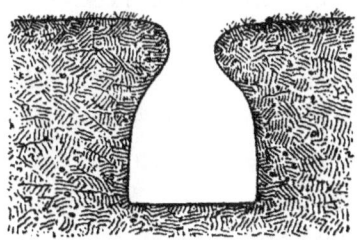

SECTION OF BOER TRENCH.

Of course, we only found out all this afterwards, and at the time it seemed as if nothing could live under the tremendous fire we brought to bear on the laager.

On the right bank Smith-Dorrien crept steadily forwards, with his right on the river-bank, throwing up shelter-trenches as he gained fresh ground.

It is always a pleasure to meet Smith-Dorrien, but, like other pleasures, it was one that had to be paid for. His camp was on the knoll which he had occupied on the 18th, and to reach it one obviously had to pass over his battle-ground, not a very savoury place at the best; but, as bad luck would have it (both for them and us), a large herd of cattle were grazing on it the day of the fight, just between the Boers and us. I tried many different roads in the hope of getting round them, but their carcasses were as far-reaching as their smell was penetrating. Holding one's breath was no good; it generally ended in having to take an extra deep one just where they seemed to be at their thickest. The only thing for it was to put a cigarette into one's mouth and spurs into one's horse, and thank Heaven they were not elephants.

As I have said, spades were rather scarce, and trenching was all-important, so we were only able to bury the carcasses nearest to the bivouacs, and had to leave the rest to time. Evidently, many of the animals had been put in the river-bed for safety on the day of the fight, and had been killed by our shells at the water's edge. The result of this was that a sudden flood a few days afterwards lifted them from their resting-places, and sent an ungainly procession of some 500 swollen corpses floating past our bivouac. If by chance one stuck in a shoal, it was helped forward on its journey, and our drinking-water after that held rather less of what doctors call 'organic matter.' I never heard what Methuen at Modder River Station thought of our gifts.

PAARDEBERG

The halt at Paardeberg was the first of more than a few hours that we had made since the division was formed, and we took advantage of it to apply for, and in some cases to get, the various persons and things we wanted. Among the former was an Intelligence Officer, and I had the good luck to secure Count Gleichen for this place, and Colonel Otter, commanding the Canadians, kindly let me take Lieutenant McLean, of his regiment, as 'galloper.'

Having been put together at a few hours' notice, we were short of nearly all the proper equipment of a Division, and among other things lacking was a flag, an important item as a guide for orderlies and others looking for our Headquarters. This want was supplied by Ewart, who generously sacrificed the red lining of his Staff greatcoat for the purpose, and somebody else having found some white calico, out of which a big IX was cut, the pieces were put together by our servants, and the whole, having been lashed to one of the mounted orderlies' lances, waved proudly over the disused sheep-pen which I had made my Headquarters. It was rather a patchwork, and varied a good deal from the 'sealed pattern.' Later we got a regulation one from Ordnance Store, with an Arabic 9 in black on it, and I never heard what became of our old friend. Perhaps Ewart took it to pieces and put it back inside his greatcoat.

In the small hours of the night of the 21st the Shropshires made a fine advance, and got within

550 yards of the nearest Boer trench, and, throwing fifty men across the river, entrenched themselves on the left bank, thus gaining the ground which the Argyll and Sutherland Highlanders had so gallantly but unsuccessfully tried to reach on the 18th.

On the following night the Shropshires again tried to push forward, but were unable to do so; after this, therefore, we made up our minds to trust to spade-work, and the next few days were spent by parties of the different battalions in turn lengthening and widening the trenches on both banks.

The thick scrub between us and the Boer lines made it difficult to know exactly what direction the northern trench should take; but on going to the end of it on the morning of the 26th, I found that it was clear of the trees, and looked into the west face of the Boer laager. To have carried it more to the south-eastward would only have exposed us to enfilade fire, while a turn to the north-east would have taken it, if carried on far enough, right outside the laager. I therefore made up my mind that we ought to make a fresh start from the right bank. It seemed to me that, if we could once gain the ground clear of the trees, we should have the laager at our mercy. I knew Lord Roberts was very adverse to trying an assault, so got hold of General Elliot Wood, his Chief Engineer, and went through the trenches again with him, with the result that he, too, thought that no further good could be done with the present trench. Fortified with this

PAARDEBERG

expert opinion, I went to Lord Roberts, explained the situation, and got his leave to try an advance that night.

It was the turn of the Canadians to occupy the trench, and therefore obviously theirs to make the assault. After talking over the details with Smith-Dorrien, it was settled that the assaulting party was to consist of half a battalion of that regiment, formed in two ranks, the rear one with their rifles slung and carrying entrenching tools; in the rear rank, too, were to be about thirty men of the 7th Company Royal Engineers, under Colonel Kincaid. The orders I gave were that they were to creep forward from the trench in the darkness till the enemy opened fire, and then to begin digging as hard as they could. The Gordons were to support them in the advanced trench, and in another, a couple of hundred yards down-stream, while the rest of the Nineteenth Brigade, extended to the left, was to open fire, so as to convey the idea of an attack in force and prevent the Boers concentrating all their strength on to the little assaulting party.

At 2.30 on the morning of the 27th February the party, under command of Lieutenant-Colonel Buchan, Royal Canadians, left the trench, moving steadily forward shoulder to shoulder, feeling their way through the bushes, and keeping touch by the right. At 2.55 they were met by a terrific fire from a Boer trench, which later measurement proved to be only 60 yards in front of them. The right companies, under Captains Macdonald and Stairs, got cover under a little fold of the ground by falling back about twenty yards, but the slight undulation which favoured them brought the French Company on the left to the level of the Boer fire, which, owing to the darkness, was rather high. The result was that before they could gain comparative shelter, some thirty yards back, their Commanding Officer, Major Pelletier, was wounded, and they had suffered rather severely. The trenching-party then set to work about ten yards in rear of the front rank, which lay in the open for nearly two hours at eighty yards from the enemy's trench, keeping up so hot a fire at the flashes from the Boer lines that firing from the other side grew wild.

When I say that cover was taken behind a fold in the ground, it must not be supposed that this was by any means complete protection. I do not think that the difference between the ridge and the crest was more than 18 inches; but the advantage of this slight swell made all the difference to the firing line lying down. Without it they probably could not have held their own at that short distance from the enemy; with it they not only did so, but made the Boer fire so unsteady that there were marvellously few casualties among the working party, who, standing up to dig, were, of course, pretty well exposed during the early stages of their work.

I have broken my rule of only describing what I saw myself, but as it all happened in the dark, and

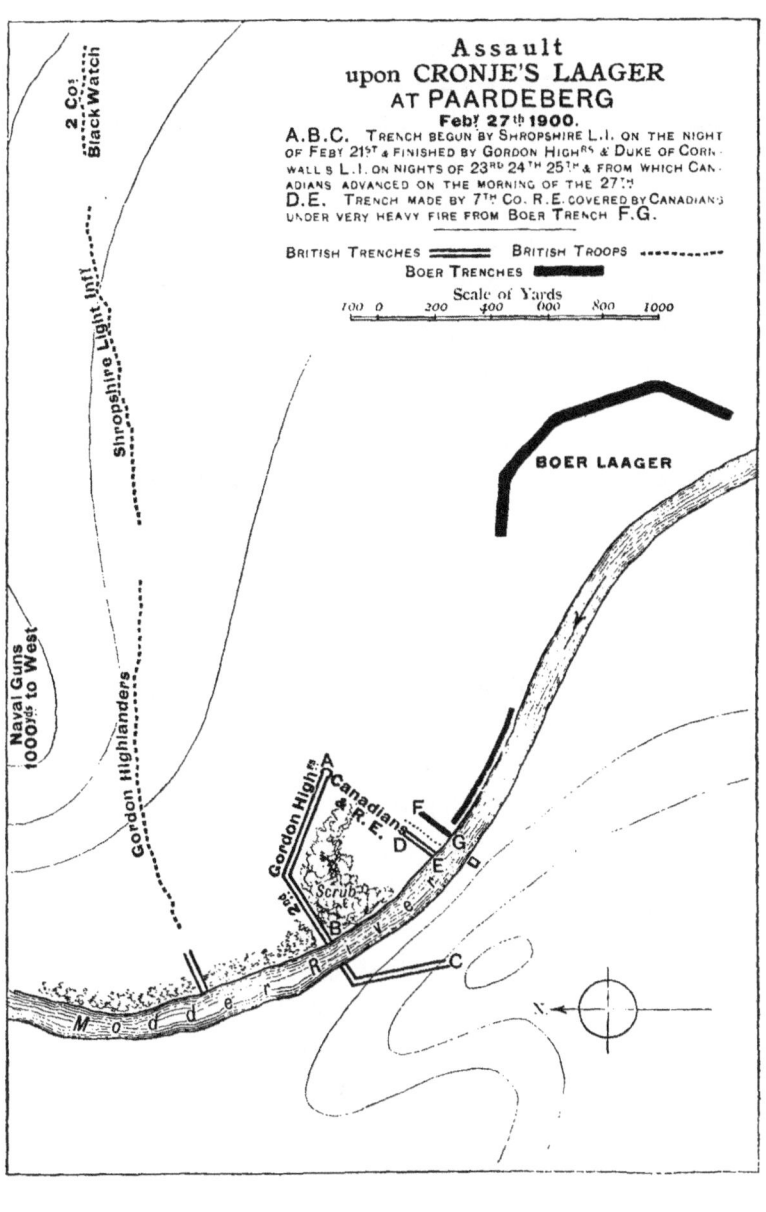

On pacing the distance between the trenches, they were found to be 90 yards apart; and we also found that our new position, besides commanding the inside of the laager, as we had known beforehand that it must do, enfiladed a trench running parallel to the river, and which protected the laager from any attack from the south. Cronje was therefore wholly at our mercy. I know nothing of what his intentions may have been beyond the Boers' statement that I have quoted. He may have intended to surrender that day or that day week, and we may not have hurried him by a minute; but whatever he may have intended, I am sure those 480 Canadians made it impossible for him to do anything but that which he did.

I left Gleichen, who had joined me as Deputy-Assistant-Adjutant-General for Intelligence, to collect the prisoners and bring them over to the south bank, and told Ewart to make arrangements for the occupation of the laager and collection of rifles and ammunition.

As the Highlanders had such a hard day on the 18th, I thought they would like to be among the first into the laager which they had tried so hard to take, and ordered that one of their battalions should march in with the Nineteenth Brigade.

I then crossed the river, got on my horse, and, galloping off to Headquarters, reported to Lord Roberts that our total casualties were forty-five, of which twelve only were killed. After saying that the attack had been very well conceived and carried out, and that the result was well worth the loss, he ordered me to have a list of the prisoners made.

Collecting the prisoners and finding out all about them gave the Staff a busy morning, and it was three o'clock before I could get the full list which Lord Roberts had ordered me to furnish. I then went off to the laager to meet him, as he had said he wished to make a speech to the Canadians and see the ground.

I had been waiting some time at the drift before he came, so got an idea of the life which the Boers must have led for the last ten days. Cooped day and night in their deep narrow trenches, out of which they could rarely have stirred, in the midst of that appalling smell, it struck me that, grand as is the devotion that makes our men stand up to the heaviest fire, there was something very admirable in the dogged determination that held these men at their posts during those ten weary days and nights, and that perhaps we are too apt to look upon our own particular brand of courage as the only genuine sort.

I am sure Ewart would have sympathized with me thoroughly, had I given vent to my views; for after his morning in the laager he was simply green, and said that he had endured all the sensations due to a storm at sea, without the consoling hope that drowning might end them.

We bivouacked that night about half a mile up-stream of the laager, and moved the next day to Osfontein, some five miles further on, where we stayed for a week while supplies were being brought up from the railway. We were all glad of a rest, and after their long spell of outpost, a mile or more from the water, it was a great boon to the men to bivouac near the river again. I, too, was exceptionally comfortable, as Nugent had got hold of a couple of covered waggons from the laager, and in one of these I was able to do my writing, without having to put away my papers every time it rained, or chase them about the country every time it blew. The story of the Paardeberg operations entailed a good deal of this, stretching as they did over ten days.

The question arose whether I should send my report separately or through Kelly-Kenny, and we agreed that it was better to take the former course, as the 18th was the only day we were together. We both took the opportunity of sending in a long list of names of officers and men who had distinguished themselves, but were told not to do it again, as these would be dealt with in a separate despatch at the end of the operations.

CHAPTER III

POPLAR GROVE

ON the afternoon of the 6th Generals of Division and Brigadiers were sent for to Osfontein Farmhouse, where Lord Roberts was staying. He explained that about 14,000 of the enemy were reported to be holding a line of trenches on both sides of the river near Poplar Grove. The Sixth, Seventh and Cavalry Divisions, Guards Brigade, and all the Field Artillery, were to work on the left (south) bank, while the Ninth Division, with three Naval 12-pounder guns and Henry's and De Lisle's Mounted Infantry, under my orders, was to look after the north side. Tucker's (the Seventh Division) was to be on my right, on the south side of the river. A sketch map was given us, showing the approximate position of the enemy, who was represented as holding a line of trenches extending for fifteen miles in a south-westerly direction from the north of Leeuwkop, a detached table-hill on the left of the ground assigned to me.

While we were at Headquarters the Division had

moved on to Makauws Drift, where I joined it, and then rode on with my Brigadiers to our outpost line, to look at the ground we had to deal with.

Before us the river meandered from the eastward through level ground, which gradually became more broken to the north and south, rising into a range of hills at about six miles to our left and three to our right. Halfway between the northern range and the river, Leeuwkop rose sheer from the plain. As usual, no Boer trenches were to be seen, but, from what Lord Roberts had told us, they evidently blocked the road on both sides of the river between Leeuwkop and the southern range.

The position struck me as a very strong one. Leeuwkop we knew to be held by the Boers with at least one gun; the ground in front of the line, where the map just issued showed the trenches to be, was flat and open, and even if we succeeded in rushing these, we should have had our flank fully exposed to the fire from Leeuwkop. This being evidently the key of the position, the only thing to do was to take it. I had no knowledge of whether the hills to the north were held or not. If they were, and the enemy was energetic, he would be able to put a force moving between them and Leeuwkop in a very awkward plight; but the Boers are so loath to leave a strong position when they have got it that I thought I might run the risk, and told Smith-Dorrien to have his Brigade under cover of some rising ground about two and a half miles west of Leeuwkop

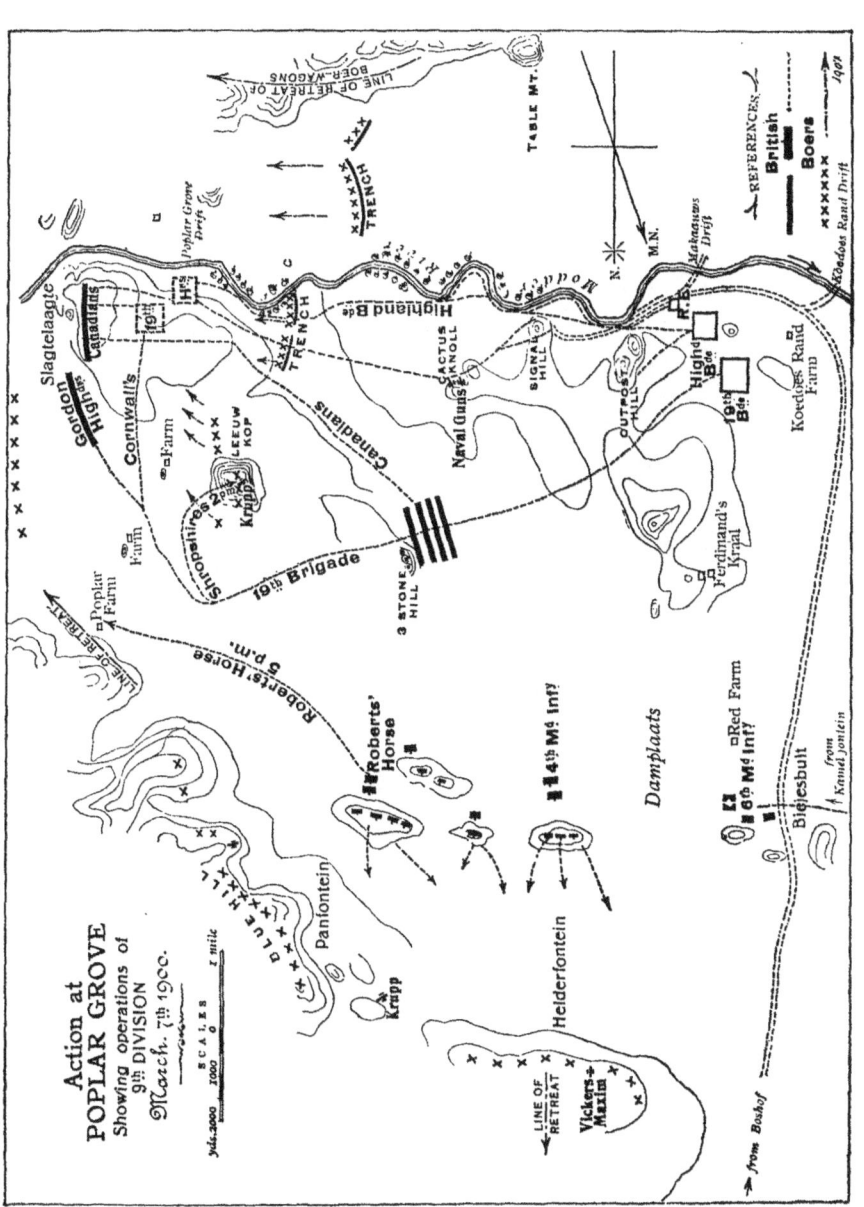

POPLAR GROVE 55

by daylight, and then work his way round the kopje, and take it if possible.

Macdonald was still in hospital from his Paardeberg wound, and Colonel Hughes-Hallett was in command of the Highland Brigade. I gave him the task of clearing the scrub by the river and holding the enemy in front while Smith-Dorrien got round the Boers' right, telling him to keep touch with Tucker on the other side of the river.

The following orders were then issued:

'OPERATION ORDERS.
'KOODOOSRAND DRIFT,
'6.3.00.

'1. The Nineteenth Brigade will march at 4 a.m. to-morrow, and, swinging its left round, will direct that left on the knoll E.N.E. of Outpost Kopje.

'2. The Highland Brigade will move at an hour to be fixed by the O.C., in time to conform with the movements of the Nineteenth Brigade, with which connection should be maintained. Its right will be rather thrown forward in the river-bed, approximately keeping touch with the Seventh Division.

'3. The M.I. will operate on the left flank of the Division, keeping up communication with the Nineteenth Brigade.

'4. The naval guns attached to the Highland Brigade will proceed to a position to be indicated by the O.C. Highland Brigade, who will detail half a battalion as their escort.

'5. The Field Company R.E. will proceed at 4.30 a.m. to the kopje now held by the Highland Brigade outposts.

'6. The transport will be inspanned by 5 a.m., and will be laagered under orders of Captain Humphreys, D.A.A.G., near the present position of the S.A.A. column. The G.O.C. Nineteenth Brigade will detail two companies as escort.

'7. The Lieutenant-General commanding will establish his Headquarters by 5 a.m. on the kopje now held by the Highland Brigade outposts.

'8. Brigade ammunition officers will place themselves in communication with Lieutenant Dyson, R.A., commanding ammunition column, who will remain with the transport laager.

'9. One day's cooked rations will be carried in the men's haversacks. Every effort must be made to-morrow to keep up supply of water to the troops, especially those remote from the river.

'INSTRUCTIONS FOR MOUNTED INFANTRY.

'The M.I. will work on our left flank, moving at 4 a.m., keeping up connection with the Nineteenth Brigade on their right, and reconnoitring the big hill to N.N.W., and occupy it if possible, and reconnoitre Leeuwkop,* sending reports to G.O.C. Division.'

* This was not done, as the officer commanding the Mounted Infantry had taken up a position in accordance with orders received direct from the Chief of the Staff, and was engaged with a force of the enemy to his left all day.

When dawn broke* on the 7th March, Smith-Dorrien's Brigade was moving on to the knoll we called Three Stone Hill, and the Highlanders were passing through the outpost line on the right. About four miles to our right front a line of Boers stood out black against the rising sun, and in front of them their animals could be seen grazing. 'They do not mean to stand,' I said to George Nugent. If I had been able to act up to that instinct Poplar Grove would have been the Ninth Division's best day ; as it was, it was its worst. It must be borne in mind that up to then the enemy had not only always stood, but had done so with the utmost obstinacy ; his position was a very strong one ; river-beds, as we knew, were his favourite haunts, and in seventeen days the Highland Brigade had not forgotten what these Modder banks had cost them at Paardeberg. We had believed that the Seventh Division would be in touch with our right, but for an hour and a half after the Highland Brigade had passed through its outpost line we could see Tucker's men still halted to our right rear, not far from our starting-place. With his right unprotected, Hughes-Hallett did not feel justified in pushing straight ahead without searching the river-banks as he advanced ; failing troops on the other bank to take alternate bends, this was necessarily a slow process, and, as the Boers did not mean to stand, gave them time to get away. As it turned

* Sunrise was at 5.56.

out, it would certainly have been better had I acted on my instinct and pushed the Highlanders straight on at the trenches, regardless of the river on one side and Leeuwkop on the other; but the map issued by Headquarters showed that these trenches stretched from the mountain to the river. Leeuwkop, we knew, was held; our right was unprotected, and I did not feel sure enough that the Boers would not stand, to risk walking into what would have been a trap had they done so.

As the Highland Light Infantry had been left at Klip Kraal, the Highland Brigade consisted of only three battalions, which its losses at Paardeberg and the wear and tear of the march had made weak ones, and it was not strong enough to detach a force to search the river and push on to the trenches with the remainder. So I asked Smith-Dorrien to let Hughes-Hallett have his right battalion, the Canadians, and with these on their left the Highlanders were able to push on rather faster.

In a very good account of this fight which Mr. Battersby wrote for the *Morning Post*, he said that the Ninth Division took its work too seriously—perhaps it did; but he made two mistakes which I should like to correct: he thought Smith-Dorrien was in command of it, and so shifted any blame there might be from me to him (*he* certainly did not deserve it); and he said that we failed to support Tucker.

I have no doubt that the Seventh Division was

doing exactly what it ought, and that it was far better employed than in helping us clear the river-banks, so I hope no one will think I am trying to throw blame on it. All that I wish to make clear is that, when the Highlanders began to advance along the river, the Seventh Division was not in front of us, and that I and my Staff, and my Sailors and Highlanders, and everyone that had eyes in his head, saw it some two miles to our right rear. As a bit of documentary evidence, I quote two extracts from the time-table kept by my Chief Staff Officer: 'Highland Brigade moved off 5.50 towards hill E. of Outpost Kopje'; '7.30 a.m. . . . General Tucker's Division still stationary.'

At 9.10 I got a heliograph message from the Commander-in-Chief that the Boers were moving their laager towards the river in rear of Table Mountain,* and that I was to push on and intercept them at the crossing, and harass their retreat. I at once ordered Colonel Hughes-Hallett to push straight on to the east, neglecting the river-banks, and passed the Commander-in-Chief's message to Smith-Dorrien, telling him what the Highlanders were doing, and asking him to co-operate as fast as he could.

At the same time a line of Boer waggons was seen retiring to the eastwards, at the foot of the southern range of hills, and Dean at once opened fire on them with his naval guns. He seemed to make good practice—that is to say, the shells fell

* This was not Leeuwkop, but a hill on the south of the river.

all among them; but I do not think any of them were disabled. They were about 7,000 yards off when he began to fire, and the range was increasing. The Boers answered him with a few shots which did no damage.

As I have said, we knew that the Boers had a gun on Leeuwkop, and on the day before it had got the range of some of our cavalry on the rising ground we called Cactus Knoll, about 2,500 yards to the north-east of the spur from which we had been firing, and 5,000 yards from the kop. I had therefore at first been rather shy of occupying this, but as some of our infantry had passed over it, and I and my Staff had been close to it without drawing any fire, I thought the gun must have been withdrawn, so decided to move on to it with the Naval Brigade, as from it we could enfilade the Boer trenches on the other side of the river. The guns were taken there without a shot being fired at them, and some half-dozen rounds had been dropped into the Boers' trenches, when the gunners on Leeuwkop woke up, and sent a shell plump into the middle of us. Dean then turned one of his guns on to the kop to answer them, and with the other two hammered away at the trenches. This was at 10.30, and the Leeuwkop gun kept up a steady fire on Dean till 11.25, by which time the trenches were empty, and, seeing that he could do no good against the gun, I ordered him to retire. I must say that I had given him leave to take up another position as soon as the gun opened on him. This was a very good instance of the harmlessness of artillery fire. The Boers had got our range to a nicety, and made excellent practice: shells dropped regularly into the battery for an hour and a quarter, yet not one man, gun, waggon, horse, or mule was touched.

This was the first of the many occasions on which I felt the want of mounted signallers; advancing, as we were, all day in a straight line, I, of course, had to change the position of my Headquarters several times, a proceeding which always rather disorganizes signalling arrangements; but it so happened that, just as the Highlanders were pushing forward, a string of messages came from various departments of Headquarters, and by the time these had been alternately ticked off and answers sent, the Highlanders had got a good start of me. If I had stayed I dare say I should have got several more, but, taking advantage of a lull, I rode off as hard as I could, telling Browne to let his men pack up their traps and follow. By the time I overtook the Highlanders the signallers on foot were, of course, far behind, and never caught us up till we finally halted. The result was that when I wanted to send a message to Headquarters I could not do so. It is true I found a man in the Seaforths who said he had once been a signaller, and volunteered to wave my pocket-handkerchief at the end of his cleaning-rod. This he did with an amount of energy which deserved success, but never called forth an answer.

When the Highlanders reached the trenches on the north side of the river they found that they had been so hurriedly left that the cooking-pots were still boiling on the fires, and most of them got a rather comforting drink of hot coffee. The enemy had retired straight to the eastwards on both sides of the river, and none of them had crossed our front, so that in any case we could not have cut off the retreat of this section of them. I do not know enough of the position of our troops to the south of the river to say whether, had we been quicker, we could have driven the Boers in the southern trenches back on to them; but 'once bit, twice shy,' and after Paardeberg the Boers did not often wait to be surrounded.

In the meanwhile Smith-Dorrien's Brigade, having got into the plain between Leeuwkop and Blue Hill (the highest part of the range to the north), found that the latter was occupied by a force, which had come from Boshof the morning before, with one Krupp gun, one 3-pounder, and one Vickers-Maxim. Smith-Dorrien therefore asked the Mounted Infantry to clear his left flank. Colonel Henry did his best to do this, but after two hours had to retire under heavy fire. The Mounted Infantry, however, protected our left all day from the force which held the Kopjesfontein-Panfontein ridge.

Seeing that he was threatened on both flanks, Smith-Dorrien kept well in the middle of the valley, so as to be at as long range as possible from the guns firing on them from Leeuwkop and Blue Hill, and pushed steadily on till he was abreast of the north-east slope of the former. The Boers, however, did not wait to be caught in a trap, and had already hurriedly retired, leaving on Leeuwkop their gun, which was taken by the Shropshires. As this retirement was not seen, the position had to be attacked on the assumption that it was strongly held; and the fact that no Boers were found on the top does not make the assault of its rocky sides a less plucky performance on the part of the Shropshires, who expected at every moment to be met by a heavy fire.

The retirement seems to have been catching, for, for no particular reason that I can see, the enemy's force on Blue Hill then split up, the southern part returning to Boshof, and the northern moving off to the southeast, parallel to Smith-Dorrien's line of advance, and just out of his rifle-range. This was particularly tantalizing. With artillery we could have pounded them, and with cavalry we could have cut them off; but the Mounted Infantry were looking after the Boshof commando, and my field batteries had all been taken for the great artillery concentration on the other side, and I had never had any cavalry.

At about three in the afternoon the Highland Brigade reached Poplar Grove Drift, and its left was joined by the Nineteenth Brigade from the northwest. The whole force pushed on as far as Slagtlaagte ridge, from which it had a fine view of the enemy streaming away to the eastward.

It was not a very glorious day's work, and I think we might have done better than we did, but at the best a foot-soldier does not stand much chance of catching up a Boer. That without any mounted troops Smith-Dorrien should have managed to capture a gun does him the greatest credit.

I reported this haul to the Chief of the Staff that evening, and was therefore rather surprised next morning to get a heliogram from him, telling me that it was reported that the Boers had left a gun on Leeuwkop, and that I should probably find it buried there. In answer, I reminded him of my report of the evening before, and said the gun was not buried. The river was in flood and impassable, which prevented me either going over to explain in person or delivering the gun, and heliograph messages that morning were curiously at cross-purposes; so that, in spite of my continued assurances that we had got the gun, I received so much excellent advice from various sources how to get it, that I was almost tempted to take it up the hill again, bury it, and then see which way of finding it worked best.

On the 9th we had orders to cross over to the south bank, and be ready to march on the following morning. The river was falling, but was still very high, and it was past sunset before we were all across.

From this place the army moved on a broader front, Kelly-Kenny's Division following the river on the left, Tucker's on the right, viâ Petrusburg, while Headquarters, my Division, and the Guards Brigade were in the centre.

We started at daylight on the 10th, halting an hour for dinner in the middle of the day, and after a seventeen-miles march reached our bivouac, which had the rather ominous name of Dreifontein, just before sunset, coming into the outskirts of a heavy fight which Kelly-Kenny had had by himself, and which resulted in more dead Boers being left on the field than, as far as I know, had ever been before counted in this campaign.

Our next march, a short one of eleven miles, brought us to the very pretty bivouac-ground of Doornboom ; and one of fifteen miles on the 12th to Ventersvlei, which I see is briefly described in my diary as 'a beastly bivouac.' Soon after noon on the 13th, one month after leaving the railway at Gras Pan, we struck the Free State main line at Fererra's Spruit, about seven miles from Bloemfontein, and experienced one of those sudden lapses into civilization to which one is occasionally liable on a campaign.

At Fererra's Spruit is the country house of Mr. John Steyn, the President's brother, a soldier at Magersfontein and Paardeberg, and an attorney in Bloemfontein, at home a most hospitable host and lover of Nature. It was only in the two last of these parts that I knew him. We had been neighbours, but not friends, while he was fighting, and I never had anything to do with his legal side. His first appeal to me was to spare his trees, and his second to spare his springbok, with both of which I thoroughly sympathized. He had reclaimed this place from the veldt, planted every tree on it himself, and watched it grow, and I could well imagine the horror with which he viewed my 7,000 firewood-seeking men let loose on his estate. I did all I could to meet his wishes, and I do not think we did much damage to the trees, though from the battle which seemed to be raging in the neighbourhood I am afraid his carefully preserved herd of springbok suffered, at all events, some 'moral and intellectual' loss at the hands of the Mounted Infantry.

We spent two very pleasant days at Fererra's Spruit, and as Mrs. Steyn chatted with us in her pretty drawing-room, she managed to make us forget that we were enemies and intruders, and very grimy ones to boot.

On the morning of the 15th we marched into Bloemfontein, where I was given a house, as Divisional Generals were allowed to live in the town, so as to be near Headquarters.

There I was joined by Campbell, my second Aide-de-Camp, who, on receipt of Ewart's telegram from Modder River Station, had hurried up from Cape Town, only to find us flown; but he was advised to push on to Kimberley, and thence travel with one of the convoys going from that place to Osfontein. He got there, however, just as that route was closed, so he turned back, and made the best of his way, viâ De Aar, to Norval's Pont, to find that the railway from that place to Bloemfontein was not yet open. Having at last been found by him, I had the bad luck to lose my 'galloper,' McLean, who had hurt his knee on the march, and had to go into hospital. Although he was only with me for a very short time, it was long enough for him to do a great deal of good work. In his place I took Lord George Murray, of the Black Watch, the only member of my personal staff who escaped going into hospital, and who stayed with me till I reached England.

As soon as the line was open, tents and stores were brought up, and the ragged, weary men got rest, shelter, food, and band instruments, and but for that curse of standing camps, enteric fever, the halt at Bloemfontein would have been a very pleasant one. Clothes and boots, however, came less quickly, and although the middle part of a Highlander is always presentable, his foot-gear is no more everlasting than that of other people; while as to the trousered battalions, some of the men's nakedness would have been less striking if they had taken their rags off altogether.

CHAPTER IV

SANNAH'S POST

ON the afternoon of the 30th March I was sent for to Headquarters, and told by Lord Roberts that Broadwood, with the Second Cavalry Brigade, being pressed by the enemy near Thaba' Nchu, was retiring on the Modder River Waterworks, and that I was to march with my Division at daylight on the following morning, join him, and attack the enemy. He said that Broadwood's Cavalry Brigade would form part of my command, and advised me to use it to get round the enemy's flank while my infantry held him in front. He did not wish any infantry attack to be made, and said that we should only just come within long-range rifle-fire.

The Chief of the Staff also handed me written orders to march at daylight on the 31st to Waterval Drift, and take four days' supplies with me. The orders said that I should be joined at Boesman's Kop by Martyr's Mounted Infantry; but they did not mention Broadwood's force, or give any hint at the further operations which Lord Roberts had sketched out. I was also given a copy of a telegram from

Broadwood, announcing his intended retirement, which was the cause of our being sent off.

My mules, which were bad when we left Gras Pan, naturally did not get better on the hard work and short rations of the march, and when we reached Bloemfontein a large proportion of them were wholly unfit for work; so that when we got this order to march, we had not enough transport to take us and the four days' supplies ordered. Fresh animals were, however, scraped together, and at 5.30 on the morning of the 31st the Division marched out of its camp to the west of the town. In the Chief of the Staff's written orders he had said that Waterval Drift was twenty-one miles from Bloemfontein; but it was a very good twenty-two from our camp, and this was a long march for the first one after a fortnight's halt, especially for men whose boots were, almost without exception, in the last stages of decay. The morning was a very still one, and the day promised to be hot, a promise which it amply fulfilled; so, although we had no reason to believe that there was any special cause for hurry, we put our best feet forward in the cool of the morning, hoping to reach Boesman's Kop before the greatest heat of the day, and to do the rest of the march to Waterval Drift when the sun began to lower.

Shortly before reaching Springfield, the Headquarters of the Second Cavalry Brigade, we heard artillery fire in the Boesman's Kop direction, and I galloped on to see if anything was known of its cause. The officer in command said he had just heard that the cavalry was heavily engaged between Boesman's Kop and the Waterworks, and a few minutes later a report came in from Martyr that Broadwood had been cut up, and had lost some guns.

As the scene of the engagement was evidently beyond Boesman's Kop, there was no chance of my infantry getting on to the spot for at least four hours; but I thought that I might be able to help with my artillery, so asked the officer in command of the post if he could furnish an escort for my brigade division. He said that there was nothing left behind there but lame and sick horses, but that he would do his best, and finally scraped together a few sabres for the purpose. I then pushed on with my Staff, telling Colonel Flint, commanding the Brigade Division Royal Field Artillery, to follow as fast as he could, and sending a message to Macdonald (my senior Brigadier) that he was to take charge of the Division and bring it on. Our horses were not in the best condition, and did not travel very fast: we were also delayed by meeting several orderlies, whom we had to stop and cross-examine; so that when, at about ten o'clock, the artillery firing became very heavy, and then died away altogether, we were still some four or five miles from Boesman's Kop.

I did not know where I should find either Broadwood or Martyr, and was simply pushing on to get reliable news on which I could act as soon as possible;

so, finding no one at the foot of the kop, I told my Staff to scatter and reconnoitre, and let me know as soon as they came across anyone. I cantered on myself, in what seemed to be the straightest line, for the place where I had heard the firing, and had passed about half the length of the kop on the south side, when I was overtaken by a Mounted Infantry officer with a message from Colonel Martyr that he was on the top of the kop, and advised me to come there.

I yield to no one in my regard for the British infantry soldier; but his greatest admirers must admit that he is not a rapid mover, especially when he is taken in bulk, and I know nothing more trying to the temper than the conviction that one ought to fly when perforce one has to crawl. Had we been able, on first hearing the guns near Springfield, to move at the rate of fourteen miles an hour, we should have saved the situation, and I knew it; and the further knowledge that we could do no more than two had, I own, made me rather irritable that morning, and inclined to go ahead somewhere, if it was only for the sake of going. It is the same feeling which makes us walk on ahead towards the station when the cab ordered overnight is late, and there is a good chance of missing the train. We know that it will catch us up with the luggage, and that we are doing no earthly good; but those of us who are not philosophers mostly do it.

Therefore, when this young officer invited me to

climb Boesman's Kop, which seemed out of the way, I am afraid I answered him rather sharply and rode on. I have never seen him since, and never knew his name; but if he is still alive, and happens to read this, I hope he will forgive me, especially as I acted on his message, after all. For, on thinking it over, I remembered that Martyr was a hard-headed man and a good soldier, and that, as he knew that he was under my orders, he would certainly have come down to meet me, unless he had some good reason for staying where he was; so I pocketed my fidgets and went up the hill.

My Chief Staff Officer's time-table states that this was at 11.15, but I do not know whether this is the time of our reaching the foot or of joining Martyr; there was about a quarter of an hour's interval between the two.

On reaching the top I at once saw that Martyr was right, as there he could show me the country spread out like a map, and explain the whole situation. Below us was a treeless plain, through which ran three water-courses, merging into one some miles to our left front. Between the second and third of these, as well as on the further side of the third, which was the Modder River, hung a heavy cloud of dust, through which a stream of traffic could just be made out moving eastwards. To the right of this the tall chimney of the Waterworks could be seen through our glasses. To our right was a range of hills some six or seven miles

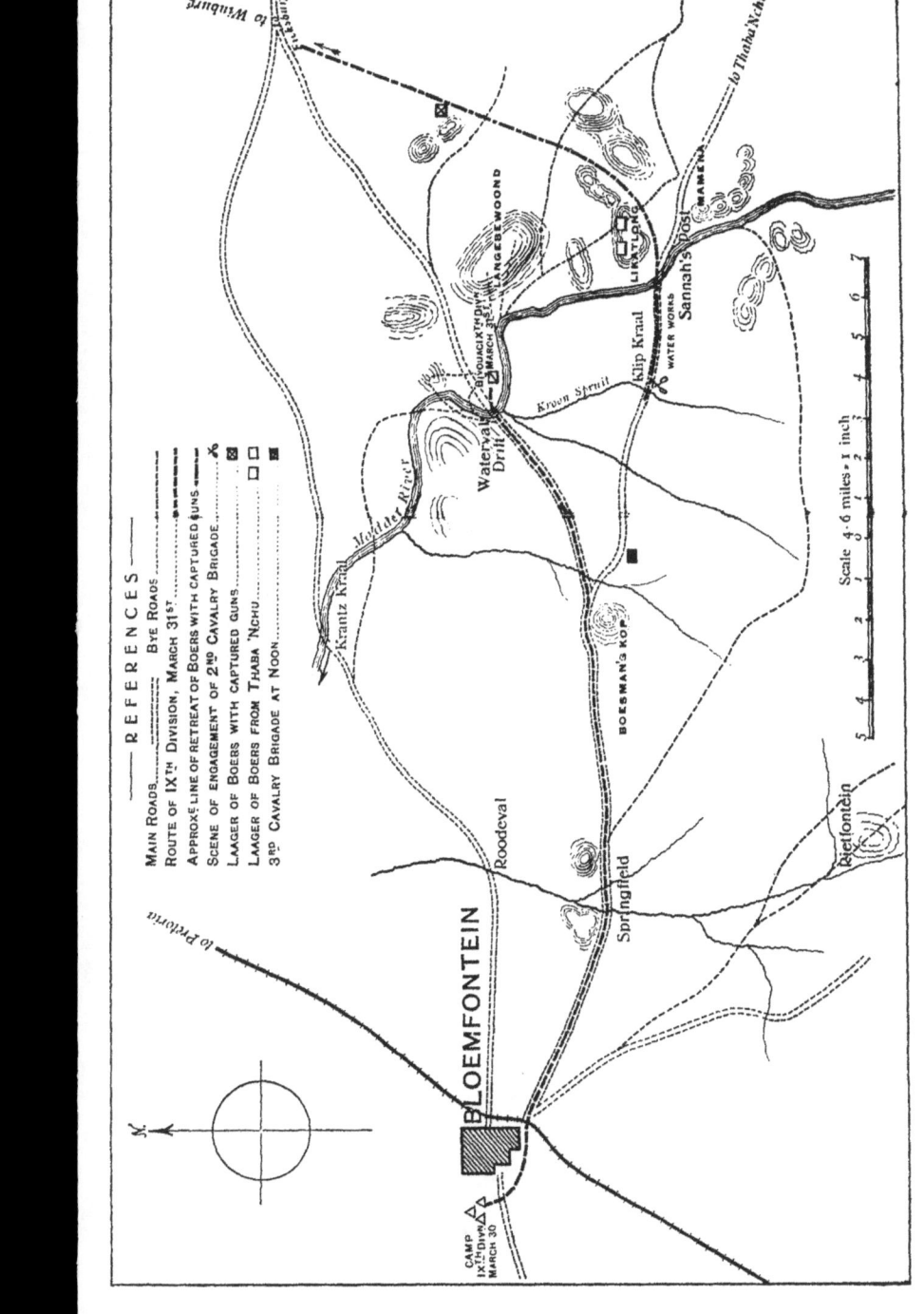

off, and another beyond the Modder curled towards the river near the point where the traffic was crossing it, and again about six miles to the north. Under this northern spur lay Waterval Drift, to which Martyr and I had been ordered to march, and which he had already seized.

No firing was going on near us, but an occasional boom from across the river, followed by a puff in the air or a little column of dust on the ground near Waterval Drift, showed that one of the enemy's guns was firing at our Mounted Infantry, which held the passage.

The Cavalry Brigade was not to be seen, being hidden by some fold in the ground; but Martyr reported that Broadwood had got clear of the enemy, and was forming up his brigade,* about two miles off, on the Waterworks road, having lost his baggage and seven of his guns.

* The watches of the Ninth Division and Cavalry Brigade Staffs must have differed slightly. Broadwood, in his despatch, says he was clear of the enemy at 11.15, the hour at which my Staff say I arrived at Boesman's Kop. As by then Martyr had had time to learn that Broadwood was forming up two miles off, this must have been done earlier than 11.15 by our time. Broadwood also says that he received the message that we were moving on Waterval Drift at two. According to the Chief Staff Officer's time-table, the Division marched off at one, and as Ruggles-Brise was sent to inform Broadwood of this before it actually moved, he could not have received it later than 1.30 by our time. I waited for Ruggles-Brise's return, but did not note the hour; but, judging from the short distance which the Division had marched before I caught it up, I do not think it could have had more than half an hour's start of me.

After the news I had had at Springfield and on the road, I had not dared to hope for anything better than this; indeed, I was prepared to hear something worse. Broadwood and his Brigade, shattered though it was, was, at all events, safe, and it seemed that our two miles an hour, which had so worried me all the morning, did not greatly matter, after all. Had my Division been mounted, it could not have got there sooner than I did, and I had not got there till the fight was over and the captured guns were eight miles off; for there was no mistaking the meaning of that stream of traffic through the dust near the Waterworks. I could not, it is true, tell through my glasses whether it was raised by guns or waggons; but a disturbed burglar does not run away with the cheese and leave the silver plate behind, and Boer human nature would have had to be very different from the usual article if it had made the enemy leave the most precious part of the capture to be taken away last. But, at any rate, the scene of the fight was six miles from Boesman's Kop, and, whether guns or waggons, there was nothing nearer to me than them except the Cavalry Brigade, safe and formed up, and the Boer rearguard between Koorn Spruit and the Modder.

The only thing to be thought of, therefore, was how to retake the guns. And I realized that, if this was done at all, it must be done by cavalry. Whether I obeyed my orders and took the direct road which led to Waterval (and incidentally 'marched on the guns,' that being the only place where there was any artillery firing), or whether I turned aside and fought my way across the spruits past the Waterworks, the Division would have covered in the first case twenty-two miles, and in the second twenty-four, before it reached the Modder. Anybody knows that if an infantry Division does anything over twenty miles in twelve hours it has not made a bad march, and at the best we could not hope to cross the river before five in the afternoon, by which time the Boers and captured guns would have had five or six hours' start of us. Over and over again the men of the Ninth Division had shown themselves ready to do all that was possible, sometimes to try more than was possible. But to have started again at the end of their forced march for another into the hills simply could not have been done, and I knew that the Modder must be our furthest point that day. If any cavalry could help, they might be able to cut into the Boers' line of retreat, and it seemed to me that it was my clear duty to secure a place from which they could act with the least possible delay.

I telegraphed to Headquarters, describing the situation, and saying I should advance as soon as my infantry arrived, but whether Lord Roberts had any cavalry to spare I did not know. I, however, had about 200 Mounted Infantry, and the remnants of Broadwood's Brigade, and I hoped that after resting all day the latter might be able to join the Mounted Infantry and push forward from the position which I wanted to secure. The whole mounted force would, of course, be weak, but they would be closely supported by the infantry, and would be reinforced by my Brigade Division Royal Field Artillery.

The next question was the choice of the place from which they could act, and this choice was obviously limited by the two drifts. In point of distance there was no great difference between them, though Waterval was the nearer of the two by a couple of miles, and, tactically, all the advantages were in its favour. To begin with, it was, as I have said, already in our hands, and there was every chance of our gaining the further bank without any fighting. But more important still was the fact that all the streams came together to the south of it, so that a force moving by the Waterval road would only have the Modder to cross, while one marching by the Waterworks would have two spruits to get over before it reached the river. Merely from the point of view of transport this was very important. Only those who have had to try it know the amount of delay that a wretched little stream can cause to a Division by making it wait for its transport, which has to halt while each waggon is laboriously dragged through the muddy bottom. But, apart from that, we who had fought at Modder River and Paardeberg well knew the almost unlimited delaying power of a few determined men armed with magazine rifles and safely sheltered in a river's bed. I did not know what rearguard the Boers would leave behind, but that they would leave one was certain—probably a very thin line at the first spruit and a thicker one at the second, which would retire on the Modder, and then hold on till dark, after which they would rejoin the main body in the hills. We need not, it is true, have made a frontal attack on these spruits, but might have swung our left round towards Waterval and taken them in flank; but this would have taken much longer than the direct march to Waterval, even without opposition, and would also have exposed our flank to enfilade from the river, on which I knew that there was at all events one* of the enemy's guns.

I therefore made up my mind to march on Waterval Drift, push across the river, and secure a position from which the cavalry could cut into the enemy's line of retreat.

Having settled this, I ordered Martyr to hold the rising ground to the north of our proposed line of advance, so as to secure our left flank, and sent my Deputy-Assistant-Adjutant-General, Ruggles-Brise, with a message to Broadwood that I wished to see him, to explain on the ground my intended movements. I waited on the kop for the arrival of the Division, and more especially for the two other Brigadiers, to whom I also wished to explain my intentions at a place from which the whole field

* As it turned out there were two.

of operations could be seen, for an ounce of ground is better than a pound of map for these sorts of explanations. I sent the message by Ruggles-Brise, a highly-trained Staff Officer, so that in case Broadwood wanted any information he would have someone who was capable of giving it clearly, and explaining all details of the situation.

Soon after Ruggles-Brise had left my artillery arrived, but seeing that there was nothing to be done on the right, unless we made a general advance that way—a plan which I had discarded—I let them rest, so as to have their horses as fresh as possible for the work which I hoped they would have later.*

Unfortunately, Grant and his Naval guns were not with me that day. Had he been, it would have been a miracle if he had not been just where he was wanted in the nick of time, and his seven-mile shots, although they would have been too late to prevent the leading guns crossing the drift, would at all events have made it impassable for the tail of the Boer convoy; but our field-guns, outranged by those of the Boers by 2,000 yards, could have done no good short of Koorn Spruit, and would have required the Division to get them there.

At about 11.40 the head of the Highland Brigade, which was leading that day, was seen approaching the foot of the kop, but it was past noon before Smith-Dorrien's Brigade had closed up. I have no

---

* As it was, they lost fourteen horses from exhaustion.

note of the hour at which the rearguard came in with the last of the waggons.

If it had been a case of pushing straight on for another four or five miles to rescue the cavalry, there is no doubt that, in spite of their hot fourteen-miles march, the men could have done it; but the Cavalry Brigade was safe,* and my only aim was to get as serviceable a force as possible into a good position east of the Modder, from which we could support a further advance. By a serviceable force I mean one which can move and is fit enough and strong enough to fight, and in thinking of the mobility of an infantry Division one has to think also of its transport. Our mules were not of the best at starting, and to have pushed on for another eight miles that hot day without watering the animals would have meant a very considerable decrease in our moving power on the morrow. Watering the transport of a Division cannot be done in much less than an hour, so, if only from this point of view, a halt was wanted. But the mule is not the only animal that wants food and rest and water. The men had been up before four, had breakfasted soon after, and had already done a good march on an unusually hot and still day. If I had pushed them straight on for another six or eight miles

* In his despatch Broadwood says he retired on Bloemfontein, because he saw that all chance of recapturing the guns was at an end, and because he had lost his kits, not because he was pressed by the enemy.

without food or water there is no doubt that my ambulances would have been full next day, and that my force would not have been so generally serviceable as it would be if I recognised that a soldier is a human being with human limitations. I may say, too, here that we had got no men to spare. We were nominally a Division (*i.e.*, about 8,000 infantry), but of the eight battalions, one—the Highland Light Infantry—had been detached before Paardeberg, and had not yet rejoined, and wounds, death, and sickness, had so reduced the rest that we were barely stronger than a full brigade—*i.e.*, about 4,200.

I therefore ordered that the transport was to be watered, and that the men were to refill their water-bottles, and eat the cooked meal which they carried in their haversacks.

I then sent for the two Brigadiers and told them my plans. Macdonald was all in favour of a stern chase viâ the Waterworks, the temptation of which was, of course, obvious. It was the one on which the cavalry had been attacked, and on which the two forces had retired in different directions; on it, though nearly eight miles away, the enemy could still be seen, and with them, presumably, the captured guns. To follow these guns, catch them up, and bring them triumphantly back to Lord Roberts, was probably the first and natural impulse of every soldier there. It would have been a very great feather in our caps if it could have been done, but, unfortunately, it could not be done—then. Had we left Bloemfontein the night before it would have been a different matter. As my orders were to march to Waterval Drift, we should have been on Broadwood's flank at dawn, and our one chance of saving him would have been to throw ourselves on his attackers; but to have thrown ourselves on their rearguard six hours later, when the captured guns were eight miles away, would have been to play the enemy's game, and waste alike time and men.

I own that I have a horror of 'councils of war,' and think that if a General does not know his own mind, he had better go home and make way for someone who does. But that is no reason why he should not listen to other people's opinions and make use of them if he can. So I listened attentively to my two Brigadiers, and was glad to find that Smith-Dorrien, a General Officer of proved judgment, took the same view that I did.

When Ruggles-Brise came back, he gave me a message from Broadwood that he was too tired to come. Having received this, and failed to get any other information from the Brigadier, my Staff Officer had first questioned some of the officers, and then ridden eastwards to the outpost line, which he found facing the Waterworks, and unmolested. He had been unable to see the retreating Boers. He reported that the Brigade was thoroughly exhausted, and would, he feared, be unfit for any further work that day.

When Martyr had sent me the message that he was on Boesman's Kop, my first thought (as I have already hinted) was that he might have reported himself at the bottom, but on second thoughts I had decided that he must have had some good reason for not doing so; but the reason which Broadwood gave for not coming to me—that he was too tired —though a very comprehensible human one after all his exertions, did not strike me as a military one at all, and as Ruggles-Brise said that his troops were too exhausted to be of use, I had to put them out of my calculations, and thought no more about it for the moment. The country was spread out before me like a map, on which I could see alike the enemy and the ground over which we should have to move, neither of which was visible from Broadwood's halting-place. He could undoubtedly have given me a most interesting account of the last six hours; but it was with the next six that I had to deal, and of what was in store for us in them I, on Boesman's Kop, was in a better position to judge than he in the plain. In his published despatch he says that he sent me a message that a direct advance on the spruit offered the best chance of assisting. As Ruggles-Brise is positive that no such suggestion was made to him, I leave it to these two officers to settle their difference of opinion between themselves. But, at any rate, the message was not delivered to me; if it had been, we should have known that opinion was equally divided, Macdonald and Broadwood being in favour of the southern, and myself and Smith-Dorrien of the northern, road; but, with all respect for Broadwood as a soldier, I should not have attached much weight to his opinion against mine in this case, for the simple reason that I was in a place from which I could see everything, and he was not.

The Division marched off again for Waterval Drift at one o'clock. Before it started I sent Ruggles-Brise again to Broadwood to let him know what we were doing, and to give him a chance of co-operating if he should find that his men were fit to do so. I stayed behind myself for a short time in case he had any message for me.

Before I left I received a telegram from the Chief of the Staff, dated 12.15, to the effect that I should push on my Mounted Infantry and guns, and do all I could to assist Broadwood. The Mounted Infantry had been pushed on by Martyr before I arrived, and had materially assisted Broadwood by extricating one of his companies from the enemy at Waterval Drift, and the guns were then going forward with the Division (I had no other escort for them).

I soon caught up the tail of the Division, which had become very long and straggly, and the sight of which made me realize more than ever that the Modder must be the extreme limit of the day's march. At about half-past two Flint came into action against the two Creusot guns on the other side of the Modder which had been firing at our Mounted Infantry, and opened fire on them; but they soon retired out of his range.

At half-past three the Highland Brigade, which was leading, came under a warm fire from the Modder River, and at the same time I learnt that Henry's Mounted Infantry had been forced to retire from the drift, so that we should have to fight our way across, after all. I could also see that a bluff to our left front, and about two miles north of the drift, was held by the Boers.

Having avoided one frontal attack, I did not want to be committed to another, even if it was only on one spruit instead of three; I therefore ordered Macdonald to ease off to his left, and move slowly, and told Smith-Dorrien, who was in reserve, to extend his Brigade, work well round to the left, and in co-operation with the Mounted Infantry to clear the bluff. At the same time I sent an Aide-de-Camp back to Flint, who had not yet come up after his engagement with the Creusots, telling him to hurry up.

While I was issuing these orders I got a telegram from Lord Roberts, which, besides telling me to do just what I was doing—viz., to make a turning movement in order to avoid being delayed at the spruits—gave the welcome news that French's Cavalry Brigade would be with me shortly, and would help to cut into the enemy's line of retreat. Although I had hoped for this as a possibility, I had not dared to do more, for I had no idea what cavalry was available. But now all seemed to be easy, and I was no longer troubled with doubts as to whether the Mounted Infantry would be strong enough or fresh enough to be of use. That the promised Brigade would be fresh when it arrived could not, of course, be expected; but, at all events, cavalry would have more go left in it at the end of a twenty-two-miles march than could be expected of infantry, and also more than the Mounted Infantry, which had been on the move since dawn. I had visions of French making a splendid dash and 'holding up' the enemy till we slower-moving foot-soldiers could come up and help him to complete the victory. But 'man proposes,' etc., and this pretty day-dream was not to be fulfilled.

In the meanwhile the Cornwalls on Smith-Dorrien's left had crossed the river beyond the bluff, from which the Boers, seeing themselves outflanked, had hurriedly retired, crossing our front within easy range of the Field-Guns. Flint got some shots into them, but the ground was a good deal cut up by dongas, into which they disappeared, and I do not think we did them much harm.

As our left swung round, the Boers gradually melted away from their right, and the Highlanders' passage of the river was hardly opposed at short ranges.

The men were all across by half-past five, and we had just time to place the outposts and settle down before dark; but getting the transport over was, as usual, a long business, and it was nearly midnight before the last waggon was parked. I was at the Waterworks drift about a month later, and found it a rather worse one than this, so that even had we taken that road, and got there with no more fighting than we had just had, our transport would have prevented us from moving on again before next morning. As a matter of fact, we should not have crossed at all, for the hills to the east of and commanding the Waterworks were seen to be thickly lined with Boers. A weak division such as ours, reaching Koorn Spruit overnight, and making a fresh start in the morning, would have had a very tough job to turn the enemy out of these hills before dark. One arriving late in the afternoon, as we should have done, at the end of a long march, would hardly have fought its way over the two miles between Koorn Spruit and the Waterworks before dark. It would have had to bivouac there for the night, commanded by the enemy on all sides, and standing a good chance of finding itself in a very awkward plight next morning. The Waterworks were practically untenable for any force which had not possession of the hills commanding them; and as things turned out, had we taken the Waterworks road (even assuming that we were not much delayed west of Koorn Spruit) we could never have crossed the Modder that day. The road we took had let us do this, and had the promised cavalry arrived the starting-point which we held would have put them in the position of being able to pursue at least twelve hours sooner than if we had had to fight all day for the Waterworks hills.

I have mentioned once or twice that the enemy with Broadwood's guns were retiring into the hills, and I have just said that the ground near the Waterworks was strongly held, two statements which seem contradictory. After the evident retirement which I had seen in the morning, the large force which I saw on Likatlong and Mamena (the hills above the Waterworks), I own, puzzled me, and has, I fancy, puzzled other people since, causing a good deal of misapprehension as to the events of the Sannah's Post day. The mystery was, however, soon partly cleared up for us by a prisoner named Fereira, whom the Mounted Infantry had taken. He said that the force which ambushed Broadwood was a comparatively small commando which had come from Winburg to attack the Mounted Infantry post at the Waterworks, and was not co-operating with the larger one, which arrived later, and was following the cavalry from Thaba 'Nchu. He was a member of the Winburg Commando, and would not say where it then was, but I had seen with my own eyes that it had retired, and I afterwards learnt from Major Burnham, who was with it as a prisoner, that it, with the last of the captured guns and convoy, crossed the Modder at noon, trekking till four, when it halted in the hills till two next morning. It then made a forced march to Winburg. It must, therefore, have crossed our front, and at that moment have been outspanned at most about eight miles to the east of us. The force which I now saw near the Waterworks was, of course, the Thaba 'Nchu one. It was evidently from this force that the 1,500 men came, whom Broadwood reported as having reinforced Koorn Spruit.*

At sunset we had still no news of French, but later I had a message from him, dated Boesman's Kop, saying he would be with me by six next morning. This did not leave me much hope that the guns would be retaken, and I telegraphed to the Chief of the Staff, explaining the general situation, and saying that I had no cavalry.

Late at night I had an answer, saying that if the enemy were as strong as I believed it would be better for me to fall back on Boesman's Kop with my whole Division, as I stood a good chance of being cut off. As I felt that I was in the best position to form a judgment on this, I took the liberty of disregarding his advice, and gave my reasons for doing so in my answer, but said I would review the situation carefully in the morning. When this came there were still no signs of French,

* Major Burnham, in his account given to the *Daily Telegraph*, says that by 8 a.m. 5,000 men were attacking Broadwood. There were fully this number in the neighbourhood, but I think Broadwood's 1,500 probably represents all who crossed to the west of the Modder, and that the remainder waited on the hills commanding the Waterworks.

and I had to make up my mind whether I should try to do anything alone with my infantry, or act on the Chief of the Staff's suggestion and retire.

A look round from our outpost line showed that the Mamena range was very strongly held by the enemy, and as any attempt at pursuit would have to begin by dealing with this force, I had first of all to settle whether that was practicable. A frontal attack would certainly have failed, and the question was whether I had enough men to hold the enemy in front and turn his flank. With a full Division I could have done it easily enough, but I calculated that I ought to have at least a couple of battalions to hold the enemy in front, and this would have only left me about 3,000 men with which to get round him—a force which, considering the ground, I did not think strong enough. I therefore telegraphed* to the Chief of the Staff, giving him my views, and saying that I should reconnoitre the position, but that unless I found the enemy much weaker than I imagined I should retire on Boesman's Kop. The answer to this came from the Military Secretary, and contained definite orders not to attack, as I was not strong enough to do so with advantage, and to retire on Boesman's Kop.

In the meanwhile, at about nine, a heavy cloud of dust had arisen on the Boesman's Kop road, which I knew must be caused by French, and which the

* Messages were sent by heliograph to Boesman's Kop, and thence telegraphed to Bloemfontein.

Boers probably thought was made by a large force, for their laagers began suddenly to break up, and in an hour's time not a waggon was to be seen.

At half-past ten French arrived with his Staff, having left his troops about a couple of miles back on the other side of the river. After riding over the ground with me, he decided that he would only be tiring his horses to no purpose if he attempted to pursue, and it was finally settled that I should leave the Highlanders at the drift to cover the passage of it by the transport while I pushed on to Klip Kraal with Smith-Dorrien's Brigade, and that French should make a demonstration towards Mamena in the afternoon. The possession of the Waterworks was a question rather of convenience than necessity —Bloemfontein could get on without them—but with them in our hands, and working, its water-supply was, of course, better. I therefore decided to retake them if I could do so without a heavy fight, but did not consider they were worth the loss of many lives.*

At Klip Kraal (the farmhouse on the west side of Koorn Spruit) I found General Porter, who with his Cavalry Brigade and four Royal Horse Artillery guns had been sent there by French to bring away some of Broadwood's wounded, and heard from him that the Waterworks and Mamena were still held

* This appears to have been Lord Roberts' view, judging from his orders to Hamilton at the end of April, quoted by Winston Churchill as follows: 'If you find the Waterworks weakly held, which is not likely, you may try to occupy them' ('Ian Hamilton's March,' p. 85).

in some force, and that his patrols had been fired at. We there learnt from a prisoner that the Boer force had split into three parts, of which one, about 1,200 strong, held the Waterworks position, while the other two had moved to the north and south with the intention of attacking Bloemfontein. If this was the case, it would evidently have been playing the enemy's game to keep my force at the Waterworks, and taking this into consideration, together with the fact that I could not hope to retake them without heavy fighting, and the Military Secretary's telegram, I at once decided to fall back on Boesman's Kop, and sent Macdonald orders to that effect.

Porter said that he wished to rejoin French, and asked me to relieve him; but as he had been put there by French for a definite purpose, and we had come there either to retake the Waterworks or retire, I did not see why I should do so, but at once acceded to his other request that I should lend him my medical officers and ambulances and waggons for the removal of the wounded. These, eighty-nine in number, were got away under the supervision of Colonel Dorman, my Principal Medical Officer, without any casualties, although they were nearly the whole time under the fire of the enemy's guns on Mamena. Whether this fire was directed on the ambulances or not I cannot say, but Porter's troops and battery were so close by, that it may have been intended for them.

I was told that the reason for removing these wounded under cover of Porter's Brigade was that the Boers claimed them as prisoners. Doubtless this was a good one, and as it was done by the order of French, who was senior to me, I simply fell in with it; but had I known what Porter was there for I should not have brought up the Nineteenth Brigade so close to him, for that body, advancing on Klip Kraal, must have made the Boers think that an attack was intended (as, indeed, it was), and it seemed to me that mixing ambulances and combatants was only putting temptation in their way.

The Boers had more than once played us tricks with white flags, and they were not guiltless of using ambulances for other purposes than the removal of wounded; but they had always treated our wounded well, and respected the Red Cross flag. During the war I had often to send in to the railway a convoy of empty waggons and a number of sick and wounded, and when this was the case took care that the two classes should be several miles apart, for fear of the convoy's escort attracting fire on the ambulances. Whether this mixture was the reason for the fire which the Boers then opened, I do not know—their Commandant may have been a man who disregarded these rules—but as no one was hit it did not much matter.

The Division concentrated at Boesman's Kop between eight and nine that evening, and on the following morning the whole force, including French's Cavalry, received orders from Headquarters to return to Bloemfontein. We halted at Springfield for the night, and reached our old camping-ground early on the morning of the 3rd April, when I at once reported myself at Headquarters.

Lord Roberts had seen Broadwood the day before, and therefore presumably knew all he had to tell, and as his only remark about our share in the work was, 'You made a capital march; I only wish I had sent you the night before,' I supposed he was satisfied with us, and went away in happy ignorance of the storm that was about to brew.

About ten days afterwards I heard rumours that I was being criticised for my action at Sannah's Post, so wrote to the Military Secretary asking if there was any truth in the report that the Chief blamed me, and in answer was told that Lord Roberts said I was not to believe in idle rumours, and that, if he had felt as rumour imputed to him, I should have been the first person to whom he would have mentioned it.

CHAPTER V

BLOEMFONTEIN TO WINBURG

ALTHOUGH the conversation with Lord Roberts, which I mentioned at the end of the last chapter, was short, as far as Sannah's Post was concerned, it lasted some time, and was chiefly on the subject of the defence of Bloemfontein. He said that he had appointed me President of a committee to draw up a scheme for this, and wanted a report as quickly as possible. It was to be based on the necessity of the force left there being small.

As soon as the members could be got together we started off, and rode up and down all the hills about the town for the rest of the afternoon, fixing positions for guns, piquets, and works, and settled to meet next day as soon as our map was ready, to read over the fair copy of the report. I had also my report to write on the work of the division on the Sannah's Post day, and was doing this when, at about eleven, I was sent for at Headquarters. Lord Roberts said that it was reported that a large meeting of Boers was to take place at Leeuwkop, about eighteen miles down the

Dewetsdorp road, on the following morning, and he wanted me, if possible, to catch them. We were to march at two that afternoon for Rietfontein, and push on early the next morning. Porter's Cavalry Brigade, with two Horse Artillery batteries, was to be attached to my command, and would, Lord Roberts thought, do most of the work, as the infantry would only be wanted to support them.

On our return from Boesman's Kop we had heard of the arrival at Bloemfontein of our much-needed boots, and had hoped to issue them that afternoon; but the order for this move gave divisional, brigade, and regimental Staffs as much as they could do, and the men had again to start off in their scraps of leather. The state of the transport, too, was, as usual, a difficulty, but, as usual, it was got over somehow, although I am afraid not in a way that was approved of by the mules.

Any chance of the expedition being a success, of course, depended on its object being kept a dead secret. I therefore only gave out that we were going to Rietfontein, and was rather surprised, when we marched off, to learn that our final destination was the common knowledge of the division.

Rietfontein, by the Intelligence Department map, was barely eleven miles from our camp, and, marching at two o'clock, we hoped to get in before it was quite dark. But men and animals were stiff, and the place was further than the map showed. The last glimmer of light had gone when the advanced guard reached a muddy little spruit running between high banks, in which waggons stuck and mules floundered in the dark, and the result was that the rearguard did not get to the place where Porter was bivouacked till past midnight. It was nine o'clock before even the head of the column reached it, and we only found it then by my Staff scattering over the country till one of them happened to hit on it; for the bivouac was in a hollow off the main road. No lights were to be seen, and it was not until Gleichen had actually ridden into it that he found out that it was there.

I do not know what may have been the experience of other Generals, but up to this it had always been mine to have cavalry temporarily attached to my division acting in the first instance under direct orders from the Chief of the Staff, an arrangement which had always proved inconvenient.

At Poplar Grove Henry's Mounted Infantry had been posted in its position and received orders direct from Headquarters; so that, although I was free to use them as I thought fit, when the work began, I had no choice as to their first position. On the Sannah's Post day Martyr had moved on Waterval Drift by order of the Chief of the Staff, and when I got to Boesman's Kop I found his troops already disposed. Now, Porter had received independent orders to march on Leeuwkop viâ Rietfontein, and had settled down in the latter place without any reference to me. As he came from Springfield, it would, of course, have been ridiculous to bring them round by Bloemfontein to join me; but had he been told that he would receive his orders from me, I should have settled some meeting-place, from which his brigade would have covered my front, and, finding out the way by daylight, have saved the infantry a good hour stumbling about in the dark.

We paraded before daybreak next morning, the main body of the cavalry pushing on to a point about two miles north-east of Leeuwkop, while their scouts searched round its base, without finding any signs of the Boer assembly. The infantry followed them in support to Paarde Kraal, and as we approached a party of mounted Boers moved out of the lower slopes of the mountain, and, crossing our front, gave the artillery with Porter a chance of firing a few shots. These seemed to fall fairly in the middle of them, but I do not think they did any harm. This party was a small commando which happened to be in the neighbourhood, and had nothing to do with the meeting.

The infantry then returned to Rietfontein, and thence next day to Bloemfontein, and the cavalry to Springfield.

Soon after this I was for the first time given some divisional cavalry, in the shape of the Eastern Province Horse; but after I had had them for about a week, they were suddenly ordered off to escort a convoy to Pole-Carew's newly formed Eleventh Division, which also swallowed up my artillery and my Deputy-Assistant-Adjutant-General, Ruggles-Brise. I was asked to part with him, as Pole-Carew had the Guards Brigade in his division, and it was said to be desirable that one of the Divisional Staff should be a Guardsman. I was naturally sorry to lose him, not only as an old friend, but a Staff Officer of the highest class; though, if I had searched the army through, I could not have found a better man than his successor, Major Cuthbertson of the Black Watch. As I think I have said before, I was exceptionally lucky in my Staff.

On the 21st April I received an order, signed 'For Chief of Staff,' that a brigade of my division was to leave at daylight next morning for Springfield to relieve the Eighteenth Brigade, which the order said would be 'moving to the eastward.' As the Nineteenth Brigade, and especially the Canadians, had suffered more from enteric than the Highlanders, Dorman thought a change of air would do it good, so I settled to send it, let the Chief of the Staff know which brigade I had chosen, and gave the necessary orders for its march. Before it started, however, there were several changes of plan; the Eighteenth Brigade, which was to have gone east to the Waterworks, was sent to the south towards Dewetsdorp, marching later than had been intended, and the Military Secretary sent me a message that the Nineteenth Brigade was to stand fast till further orders, while the Chief of the Staff sent Smith-Dorrien another, without letting me know, that he was to stand fast till eight, so we were rather at cross-purposes that morning. However, it got off at last, and, as it happened, I never saw it again.

On the 22nd I heard that Major Long, my Transport officer, had been told that the Chief of the Staff would inspect the Divisional Transport next morning. As the Nineteenth Brigade had gone, there was only that of the Highlanders left; but I suppose it was looked upon as representative, for next day I received a memorandum from the Chief of the Staff saying that the Field-Marshal Commanding in Chief regretted to learn that my transport was not in an efficient state, the animals having been overworked and not allowed sufficient rest and grazing. He added that this state of affairs appeared to be due to want of supervision, and I was referred to an Army Order on this subject which had been issued on the 13th February. I was ordered to report in a week's time on the state of my transport, and say what steps I had taken to make it efficient.

On the same day Major Long received a memorandum from the Director of Transport saying much the same thing, but adding that it was Long's business to see that the mules were attended to, and that, unless they improved, his fitness for his appointment would have to be considered.

Even among the Staff of the Ninth Division Long was conspicuous for his hard work and enthusiasm. The care of mules was not only his 'business,' as the Director of Transport put it, but his hobby, and if he had a fault, it was a tendency to worry everybody, including the Headquarter Staff, about the condition of his animals. I was therefore very indignant at this attack on him for a state of affairs for which neither he nor any member of the Divisional Staff was responsible.

The Army Order quoted pointed out that waggons should not be overloaded, and that animals should be turned out to graze when possible, that Transport officers should report on the condition of the animals daily, that Regimental officers should be appointed to assist the Transport officer, and that an officer should be detailed to superintend the passage of drifts. With regard to these, if the waggons were overloaded, it was not our fault. We were ordered to march from Enslin with a certain amount of equipment and a certain number of days' supplies, and given a certain number of waggons and mules to drag them. As I have already said, we had not gone many hundred yards on our first day's march before we found out that the loads were too heavy for our wretched beasts, and I had to lighten them by dropping greatcoats. The order to turn out the animals to graze had been carried out to the letter, though circumstances had interfered with the fulfilment of its spirit, especially during the ten days' halt at Paardeberg, when the concentration of the army on a few square miles of already dried-up veldt had soon removed the last vestiges of vegetation. Long had regularly reported on the condition of the animals, and his report had always been the same—that they needed food and rest, and if they did not get them they must invariably break down. Regimental officers had been detailed as ordered, and one or more of the Divisional Staff had stayed at each of the many drifts* we crossed till the last waggon was over, this often not being till past midnight. We had therefore got clear consciences about this. All the animals were exhausted when we arrived at Bloemfontein, and I had reported that 302 of them wanted thorough rest to make them fit for work at all, and both Long and I had sent in reminders of their condition. The remainder would probably have pulled round if they had been given a chance, but the two marches to Waterval and Rietfontein, with the heavy drift work they entailed, had put them back terribly. Even when we were resting, drawing wood kept eighteen waggons a day employed, as none was allowed to be cut nearer to Bloemfontein than Quaggafontein, eight miles off. Stores, too, had to be got up from the station, and supplies drawn for the division, and a number of men attached to it. Although we, of course, used the fittest animals for these purposes, even they were badly in want of rest, and it was a source of wonder to me, not that many of the mules were in bad condition, but that Long should

* We had crossed the Riet River once, the Modder four times, besides several smaller streams which proved quite as trying to the transport as the larger rivers.

have managed to have so many who could work at all.

In my answer to the Chief of the Staff I expressed my regret that the Commander-in-Chief should not have been made acquainted earlier with the condition of my transport; drew attention to the facts which I have just mentioned; pointed out that some of our worst animals were among those recently issued from the Remount depôt; and that, in spite of all our hard work and short rations, my transport was more efficient than it was at the date of the mobilization of the division, and that it reflected the greatest credit on Major Long and all concerned that the division had marched into Bloemfontein with the whole of its vehicles.

The only immediate reply to this was a memorandum from the Director of Transport, informing me that Colonel Johnson, Royal Garrison Artillery, had been ordered to report himself to me to take over the duties of Senior Transport Officer from Major Long.

On hearing that he was to be superseded, Long applied through me for a court of inquiry, as he protested against the charges which had been brought against him, and considered that he had been made a scapegoat, in order to account for the bad condition of the transport.

The answer to this demand was a telegram from the Director of Transport, sent some ten days later, in which, after refusing Long's request for a court of inquiry, he said that the Chief recognised the difficulties under which, in common with other divisions, we had laboured with regard to overwork and scarcity of forage, but that Lord Roberts trusted that every care would be taken to keep the animals as fit as possible.

Long was neither reinstated nor removed, but remained till the division was broken up, working as hard and as loyally as ever, and giving his successor the full benefit of his experience; for Johnson, a capital fellow, a keen soldier, and expert Artillery officer, had an extensive knowledge of elephants, horses, camels, and traction engines, not to mention big guns, but happened to have had nothing to do with mules till he joined us. He had come out in charge of a battery of 5-inch guns, and as these either were not wanted or could not be got up to the front, he was placed in charge of our transport.

On the afternoon of the 23rd (the date of the transport memorandum) I had a note from Kitchener asking if I would come and see him next day, and answered, fixing an hour. At nine on the same evening I received an order signed by one of the Staff 'for Chief of Staff,' that I was to march next morning for Springfield with the Highland Brigade and two Naval guns in support of the Nineteenth Brigade, then at Boesman's Kop. The order said that we were to take three days' rations, but were not to wait for either guns or baggage, which could follow under an escort. At 9.30 Colonel Cowan, the Military Secretary, came to see me, bearing a memorandum signed by Lord Roberts, which, after informing me that Ian Hamilton with a portion of the Mounted Infantry was in possession of the Waterworks, and the Nineteenth Brigade had been ordered to support him, said:

'The Highland Brigade will march to Springfield, and be prepared to move at once should General Hamilton require their assistance. In the event of no orders awaiting them at Springfield, they will at once proceed to Boesman's Kop, and endeavour to open communication with Generals Hamilton and Smith-Dorrien.

'Failing communication with them, or if the troops in front are heavily engaged, the Highland Brigade must advance at once to their support. It is essential that the Waterworks should not again fall into the hands of the enemy. Keep me informed by telegraph from Springfield what goes on, and beyond that by heliograph.'

As this seemed to point to rather a critical state of affairs, and as no date for marching was mentioned, I asked if the order was for an immediate start, but Cowan said that next morning would do.

We were off at daybreak on the 24th, and, hearing nothing at Springfield, pushed on to Boesman's Kop. There I heliographed to Hamilton and Smith-Dorrien as ordered, and, as all seemed to be quiet to the front, waited a couple of hours for an answer, but, receiving none, marched on to Klip

Kraal (Koorn Spruit). There I got two telegrams from Headquarters, the first, unsigned, saying: 'You should remain at Boesman's Kop with Macdonald's brigade. Should General Hamilton require support, you should send any force he may ask for and report here. Keep General H. fully informed with what troops you can supply him, his troops arrived at Boesman's Kop.'

This rather cryptic message conveyed the idea that my anonymous correspondent looked upon me as a master of legions, and that out of my abundance I should send Hamilton any troops he wanted except the Highland Brigade. Two sentences were, however, clear. In the first place, this order cancelled the one, on which I had acted, to push on from Boesman's Kop if I failed to get into communication with Hamilton or Smith-Dorrien, and, secondly, I was to communicate with the latter again. This I did, and, as my whole force consisted of three battalions, I could only tell him that they were at his disposal.

In answer he said that he required no reinforcements, that he had no instructions to push on, but that if he did Smith-Dorrien could fully hold his own. It was therefore evident from the Bloemfontein telegram that we were in the wrong place, and from Hamilton's message that we were not wanted; and having grasped this, I felt that I had done enough for one day, and went to sleep. I was, however, soon aroused by my Aide-de-Camp handing me a telegram from the Military Secretary, addressed both to Hamilton and myself, telling us that French, telegraphing from Groetfontein Farm, said he intended to cross the Modder on the following day 'to Thabacho Dewetsdorp, ready to hem in force in front of Rundle.' It added that French feared the enemy would 'give him the slip during the night. Enemy opposing him to-day retired N.E., apparently towards Thabacho. Telegraph your plans and proceedings.'

I do not know what 'general idea' may have been given to Hamilton, but the whole of my information, either as to Lord Roberts' plans or the disposition of the army, was contained in the orders on which Smith-Dorrien's and Macdonald's Brigade had marched. The first had told me that the Eighteenth Brigade was moving to the east, and although it was common knowledge in Bloemfontein that it had gone south, the original order had never been modified, while from the last I had learnt that the Mounted Infantry Division and Nineteenth Brigade were at the Waterworks. I therefore opened the map and looked for Groetfontein, and, finding one of the many places of that name on the Bloemfontein-Constantia road about nine miles north of Dewetsdorp, assumed that was the one from which French had telegraphed, and that if he was trying to cut off a force moving from the south, the sooner someone got on to the Thaba 'Nchu-Ladybrand line the better.

As Hamilton and Smith-Dorrien were already ahead of me, and were in a position to get their transport over the Waterworks Drift at once, they had not only an hour's start of us in point of distance, but three or four in point of time, and they were obviously the people to push on first. I therefore telegraphed to the Military Secretary :

'Suggest that Hamilton and Smith-Dorrien should move to Thaba 'Nchu, Macdonald relieving them at Sannah's Post, leaving two companies at Klip Kraal. Please telegraph if approved. Consider it would be better if whole division could go on, and another brigade take Macdonald's place.'

I sent a copy of this to Hamilton, and hearing later that the first part of it was approved, let him know, and got off at daylight next morning, so that his force should not be delayed by having to wait for us. I reached the Waterworks at half-past seven, and there found Hamilton getting ready to start. Supply difficulties and one thing and another, however, delayed him a good deal, and it was ten o'clock before the Mounted Infantry Division and Smith-Dorrien's Brigade moved off. Five hours later I received a message from the Chief of the Staff, ordering me to relieve the latter, as it was to march to Thaba 'Nchu.

Up to this Boesman's Kop had been the telegraph terminus; but in the afternoon the Engineers brought the line on to us, and for the next few days my signallers were kept hard at work passing messages to and from Hamilton.

Sannah's Post was also made a supply depot for the Thaba 'Nchu district. We were reinforced by the 87th Howitzer Battery, and what with orderlies, Staff and Departmental officers, and Correspondents, we had a fairly constant stream flowing backwards and forwards through our bivouac, and the neighbourhood of the lately deserted Waterworks became quite a busy one.

We had originally been ordered to march to Springfield (six miles from Bloemfontein) with three days' supplies; and although the possibility of our going further had been mentioned in the order, we had had no reason to suppose that this trip would be a longer one than the others we had made from Bloemfontein, or that we should not have a chance of reclothing the men and completing various items in which we were still deficient. We also marched as light as possible, leaving all our heavy baggage under a guard in camp. When the three days lengthened into six, and there seemed to be signs of a general forward movement, I tried to find out whether we were likely to return to Bloemfontein and advance up the railway, or strike north from where we were, but heard nothing till the 29th, when I received the following :

"'G.O.C. 9TH DIVISION, WATERWORKS.

'April 29 Q. 782.—The following orders have

been sent to G.O.C. 7 Divn and 21 Brigade. Begins: "After the operations to-morrow, General Bruce Hamilton's Brigade will move to Kaalfontein, and Genl Maxwell's Brigade will hold the Vlokfontein Schantz Kraal Ridge. The batteries of the 7th Division will remain with that Division, and two Field Batteries and two 5-inch Guns which are proceeding to Krantz Kraal to-night will join Genl Bruce Hamilton's Brigade at Kaalfontein after the operations, these latter have orders to report to-night to General Maxwell at Krantz Kraal, and will be utilized by him during to-morrow's operations. One of these field Batteries will be subsequently sent on by General Bruce Hamilton to join General Smith-Dorrien's Brigade in the neighbourhood of Morago. General Broadwood's Brigade will bivouac with the 21st Brigade at Kaalfontein on the evening of the 30th. The Highland Brigade will leave a Battalion at the Waterworks, and will move to Watervaal Drift on the 30th, when it will be joined by the Highland L I and a battery of Artillery. A copy of this will be sent by mounted orderly from the Glen to General Maxwell. Acknowledge receipt." Ends. G.O.C. 9 Division will issue the necessary orders for two Battns of the Highland Brigade to move with the 4·7 guns to Watervaal Drift to-morrow, and will send orders to Boesman's Kop, telling the Battery of Artillery which reaches there to-night at what hour it should start to meet him at Watervaal Drift to-morrow. The Head

Quarters of the 9th Division will also move to Watervaal Drift to-morrow, one Battalion and Howitzer Battery being left at the Waterworks. General Smith-Dorrien's Brigade will move to Morago under orders of Genl Ian Hamilton.

'CHIEF OF STAFF.'"

In a later telegram of the same date, the Chief of the Staff said: '"The present six Divisional Artillery is detailed to join you vide instruction in my Q. 982 of this date. The 82 Battery is now marching to Boesman's Kop the 76th and 81st, under Lt.-Col. Waldron, are proceeding to Krantz Kraal to-night."'

The move actually ordered was not a very great one, and I was leaving a battalion and a battery behind; but, on the other hand, the allusion to 'operations to-morrow' showed that some movement was going to take place near us. We were to regain our long-lost Highland Light Infantry, which Macdonald had had to part with in the middle of February, and, as far as I could make out, my brigade division, which had gone to the Eleventh Division, was to be replaced by another from the Sixth.

CHAPTER VI

BLOEMFONTEIN TO WINBURG (*continued*)

WE marched to Waterval Drift on the 30th, and there I had a telegram from the Chief of the Staff telling me that the battalion we had left behind would be relieved by one from the Sixth Division, and that the Highland Light Infantry, with drafts, my Divisional Cavalry, and the remainder of my Field Company Royal Engineers, would join me next day, and that 'the Highland Brigade should be prepared to move forward, if necessary.' This last instruction had been carried out in anticipation for some time past as far as the matter lay in our hands, for the whole brigade was chafing to get forward, and we had all worked our hardest to be ready for the advance when it came. We were however, still deficient in many things; we had no Field Hospital, only one medical officer besides the P.M.O., we were short of small-arm ammunition-carts, and many of the men had not yet got their new clothing. Of course, all this had been reported before, and I reported it again; but it was not till we reached Ventersburg, three weeks later, that we got our Field Hospital, and the men were finally clothed and booted.

On my telling him of this telegram, Macdonald sent his Aide-de-Camp, Captain Wigham, into Bloemfontein to try and make arrangements on the spot for our necessities being sent out. He came back with a message for me from the Chief of the Staff that we were to march next day by the road leading north-east from Waterval to where it crosses the Bloemfontein-Clocolan road, and there take up a position on the most suitable ground. This point was shown on the map as close to Morago, to which Smith-Dorrien was moving, so we all hoped that by the evening of the 2nd the division would once more be united. The arrival of the Highland Light Infantry would complete the Highland Brigade, and the Cavalry, Artillery, and Engineers promised would make up our complement of divisional troops; we were going to effect a junction with the Nineteenth Brigade, and everything looked very promising. I would rather have had my own batteries back, and was sorry that Kelly-Kenny should have had to give up all his artillery and one of his battalions for us, for our divisions had fought side by side at Paardeberg, and I hoped that they might do so again at Pretoria.

The Chief of the Staff's telegram had said that the Highland Light Infantry and Eastern Province Horse would join us on the 1st; but late in the afternoon I had a message from Colonel Kelham, commanding the Highland Light Infantry, that his advance-guard had only just arrived at Boesman's Kop, that his rearguard and baggage would not get in till seven, and the drafts were not fit to go on, and asking whether they could halt there for the night. As our orders from the Chief of the Staff were to march early next morning, it seemed likely that they would never catch us up if they were left behind, so I said the battalion must come on, but the drafts, with a proper proportion of officers, could follow at daylight next day. The battalion got in soon after ten, and marched with us next morning, fairly fresh, and the drafts just out from England struggled after us, not joining us till after dark.

The squadron of Eastern Province Horse was also a good deal the worse for wear. It had been sent from Bloemfontein, as I have already said, to escort a convoy to the Eleventh Division, and having done that, Captain Higson, the commanding officer, said it had been used to round in cattle, making some very long marches; then it had been suddenly recalled to Bloemfontein, and packed off to rejoin me in such a hurry that there was not time to provide either transport for the baggage or rations for men and horses. None of the latter were fit for hard work, and a large proportion of them not fit for any work at all.

We marched at six on the morning of the 2nd May, and were within a couple of miles of our intended halting-place, when I heard shots to our right front, and presently an Eastern Province Horse orderly galloped up with a message that there was a large Boer laager to our front, and that our cavalry was engaged with the enemy on the range of hills to the south-east. I knew that Maxwell's, Bruce Hamilton's, and Broadwood's Brigades were somewhere to our left, and that Smith-Dorrien was due at Morago, but he might not have got there. If he had not, this reported enemy was between him and us, and we stood a good chance of making a haul. However, I did not feel very confident about it, and sent a message to Higson to find out for certain who they were, and rode on myself to a kopje, from which a large bivouac was visible about 6,000 yards to the south-east. The haze made it difficult to make out details, but it had not the look of a Boer laager; on the other hand, the fire which was being kept up on our cavalry did not point to its being friendly. So I sent for the artillery. The Field Battery was useless till the other side advanced; but the bivouac was within nice range of Grant's guns, and I could see that he was itching to drop in a shell or two. In the meanwhile some bold Eastern Province man had got near enough to our opponents to learn that they belonged to the Mounted Infantry Division, and having persuaded them that all is not Boer which wears a slouch hat, the firing ceased, and by noon the greater part of the force had settled down in its bivouac. It was night, however, before the last of the poor footsore drafts had struggled in.

Up to this morning, when the divisional troops had marched with us, our force had consisted of three battalions of the Highland Brigade, under command of their own Brigadier, with full Brigade Staff, and myself with the Divisional Staff of some thirteen officers. Had the Highland Brigade been detached, Macdonald would, of course, have been in direct communication with Headquarters, have made his own plans for carrying out orders, and would have had full responsibility. If, on the other hand, the division had been complete, he and the other Brigadiers would have had general instructions from me, the details of which they would have carried out on their own lines; but a large Divisional Staff with only one weak brigade to look after made a situation awkward for everybody.

I think we all tried to avoid interfering with the Brigade Staff work as much as possible, but it could not be altogether helped. For instance, in the ordinary case of the orders for a march, the Chief Staff Officer would write: 'The Division will march to-morrow at such and such an hour; such a Brigade will furnish the advance-guard,' etc. The two Brigadiers would then issue their own orders for the parade of their brigades. But with the whole division consisting of three battalions, two guns and about fifty sappers, I either had to make up my mind to do nothing but accept the responsibility

8—2

for anything that went wrong, or else issue divisional orders which dealt with Macdonald's battalions. As an instance of this, I give the actual orders issued for the march to Waterval.

'DIVISIONAL ORDERS.
'WATERWORKS,
'April 29. 5.30 p.m.

'1. The Divisional Staff, the Naval Brigade, two battalions of the Highland Brigade, and 7th Co. R.E., will march to-morrow morning to Waterval Drift.

'2. 1 battalion of the Highland Brigade and the 87th Howitzer Battery and detachment Kitchener's Horse, under Lieut.-Colonel Hughes-Hallett, D.S.O., will remain to defend the Waterworks. This force will be disposed as follows : 6 co^s and 4 guns on Mamena, 3 co^s and 2 guns at the Waterworks. The 4 guns referred to should relieve the Naval guns on Mamena at 7 a.m. to-morrow. This force will move off from the Waterworks at 9 a.m. in the following order :

'1$\frac{1}{2}$ battalions Highland Brigade.
'Naval Brigade.
'Royal Engineers.
'S.A.A. Column.
'2nd Line Transport.
'$\frac{1}{2}$-battalion Highland Brigade as rearguard.

'3. Two days' reserve, in addition to to-morrow's rations, and forage will be carried.

'The men will carry one blanket on them.

'4. The Klip Kraal detachment will join the Column on the march.'

These orders left to the Highland Brigade Staff the task of fixing the hour of parade, etc., naming the battalions to lead and furnish the rearguard, and making the necessary arrangements for the Klip Kraal detachment to join at a convenient point on the road; but, on the other hand, it necessarily interfered with the internal arrangements of the brigade.

I think we all did our best to make a false position as bearable as possible, but it must have been quite as irksome to Macdonald as it was to me, and I was therefore not surprised, soon after we halted, to get a note from him saying that now I had overtaken my other brigade and my brigade division, and was in command there, he hoped the rôle of rearguard, hitherto that of the Highland Brigade, had come to an end. In this hope I heartily joined, but had not had time to answer his letter before the following telegram was handed me from the Chief of the Staff:

'G.O.C. 9 Div., Fair Field, viâ Jacobsrust.

'May 2 Q. 913.—The following orders have been issued to Gen Hamilton and the G.O.C. 2nd Cavalry Brigade, 19th Brigade, and 26th Brigade. Please comply with them. The 2nd Cavalry Bde, 21st Brigade, and 19th Brigade, with a Brigade

Division R.F. Artillery and two 5-inch guns, the whole under command of General Ian Hamilton, will march under the orders already given to that officer by the Field-Marshall C.-in-C. The Head Quarters of the 9th Division, together with the Highland Brigade and two 4·7 guns, will follow General Hamilton's column by the Winburg Road, remaining some 5 or 10 miles in rear of them, so as to be available on either flank or as a support if required. Acknowledge receipt.

'CHIEF OF STAFF.'

The first thing to do after reading this was to hand over the newly-joined field battery to Hamilton, the second to calm my Staff with apt quotations from the Book of Job, and the third to try and find out what it was all about. In this last I failed, and although I got an inkling of it a fortnight later at Winburg, I never learnt the answer to the riddle till the end of June, when Lord Roberts told it to me at Pretoria.

In the meanwhile we did not even know where we were going. We knew, it is true, that we were rationed up to the night of the 4th, and that we were to march some five or ten miles in rear of Hamilton. As he was on the Winburg road, there was some probability that he might lead us to that place, but I had no idea what his orders might be, or whether we were to follow him indefinitely or not.

However, there was nothing to be gained by

BLOEMFONTEIN TO WINBURG

guessing, and there was one comfort in the situation, that, as we had to let him go ahead, the sore-footed men, who had just made a forced march from Bloemfontein, would have a short one the next day, at all events. With reference to these and our other requirements, I telegraphed to the Chief of the Staff:

'About half the waggons of the Highland Light Infantry have broken down, the pipe-boxes having broken, and can only proceed empty. Please replace them as early as possible. 100 men of the H.L.I. are unfit to march, being footsore. I have no means of carrying them, and ambulances are urgently required. About 50 of the E.P.H. are dismounted, owing to their horses having broken down from last week's work with the 11th Division. Their blankets and kit have not yet arrived.'

Hamilton marched at six next morning, and we, after giving him a three hours' start, marched to Papjes Valley, about six miles to the south of his bivouac at Verkerdes Vlei. Here the patrols brought in a man, whose statement I passed on to Hamilton in the following message:

'MAJOR-GENERAL HAMILTON, C.B.

'May 3., 3.50 p.m. No. 56.—A Jew, named Druyn, brought in by my patrols, reports about 1,400 Boers a little to the east of New York. He is positive that President Steyn is with them. He also reports that about 600 of this force, which was originally 2,000 with 6 small guns, moved towards Winburg this morning. If you propose to take any action on this which may affect me, please let me know, also where you propose to march to-morrow.'

'PAPJES VALLEY.'

In answer, Hamilton sent a memorandum to my Assistant-Adjutant-General, saying that he had seen some thousand Boers crossing his front to occupy a big hill to the north, about two and a half miles off, behind which he had also seen another body of the enemy moving, apparently to occupy some passes and broken ground. He added: 'I must, of course, dislodge these people, and hope to be able to do so by a wide turning movement, but the place looks an ugly nut to crack. If General Colvile would make an early start to-morrow morning, he would probably arrive during the fight, and would judge for himself what he had best do. With the enemy astride my path, I cannot, of course, say when I will be able to march to-morrow.'

I had a look at the ground from our bivouac, and it certainly seemed to justify Hamilton's estimate of it as an ugly nut to crack. Immediately in front of us and to our right was an open plain. Some seven or eight miles to our right front a high black hill, as far as I could see, steep and rocky; to the right of this a range of lower, irregular-shaped hills stretching away towards the eastern horizon. To the left of the big hill a ridge, probably some 200 feet high, behind which rose another and higher range, which seemed to curl round to the west and join into the broken ground which cut the sky-line three or four miles to our left.

By the map Winburg lay straight behind the big hill, and, as Hamilton did not say whether his turning movement would be to the right or left, I could not be certain whether he would make his way between the big hill and the range to the north or through the group of kopjes to the east of the former. I could see this group, and it looked bad; but I could not see the other, and it might be worse. However, the enemy's line of retreat would certainly be to the north, and it therefore seemed most probable that Hamilton would try to work round their right. If we had had a telegraph instrument with us, all these questions would have been easily settled. Hamilton had a Telegraph Detachment, which laid down a field line as he went, and he was in constant communication with Headquarters. As we followed him, this line generally ran through our bivouac, but, having no instrument, our only means of communication with him was by heliograph or orderly. It so happened that the ground rarely allowed us to heliograph to each other, and an extra twelve or fourteen miles a day was too much to ask of my few worn-out Eastern Province horses if they could possibly be saved it.

We moved off about half an hour before sunrise

on the morning of the 4th May, and as day dawned saw that nothing was going on to our right, so it was evident that Hamilton was making his turning movement to the left. The map showed that the road turned to the eastward after Verkerdes Vlei, and I therefore thought that by marching to that we should find ourselves a little to the rear of Hamilton's right. This proved to be the case, and on reaching the top of the ridge to the north of the vlei we could see his troops extended across the undulating country which lay between us and the high range we had seen from our bivouac, and facing a lower ridge which connected this with the big hill. This latter we now saw was a tablemountain of the class so common in South Africa, with steep rocky sides scored by deep kloofs. Its base was an irregular square, some twenty miles in circumference, and its flat top, as we afterwards learnt, about four miles across. It stood some 500 or 600 feet above the surrounding country. Gleichen learnt that its name was Babiaansberg, or Baboon Mountain. Running towards this in an easterly direction, but dying away about two miles short of it, was the ridge on which I stood.

The field of battle was therefore in a hollow square formed by the four ridges, with Babiaansberg standing like a turret in the south-east corner, this and the eastern wall being held by the enemy.

At this moment Hamilton's troops were advancing towards the eastern ridge with a squadron of

Roberts' Horse on their right flank, to the south of the mountain; and my men were at the foot of the southern ridge, facing north.

In his message of the night before Hamilton had said that Babiaansberg was being occupied by the enemy, but I could not see whether they still held it; if not, we should probably have little to do; and if they did, it looked as if we should have quite as much as we wanted, for, with his troops so far to the left, it was evident that if anybody tackled it, it must be us. I told Browne, my Divisional Signalling Officer, to try and get into communication with Hamilton, and sent word to Macdonald to feel his way towards the mountain, overlapping it with his right, as far as he could extend, but only to act as a containing force till we had further information. Some delay was caused by having to wait for the signallers, and it was 9.15 before we got into communication with Hamilton, whom I informed of my position and intentions. By this time we could see that Babiaansberg was held, and, the Highland Brigade having changed front and fairly begun to advance, I ordered the Naval guns to take up a position towards the eastern end of our ridge, and told Grant to let the Boers have a round whenever they gave him a good target.

By eleven the Highlanders had reached the foot of the hill—the Black Watch on the left, next the Highland Light Infantry, and the Seaforths on the right, round the southern side of the south-east spur.

The enemy in some force was clearly seen in a kloof straight above the Black Watch, and on the summit above the Highland Light Infantry. At 11.15 Macdonald wrote :

'As far as I can make out, the hill is very heavily held, and I am at present containing them in front because it will involve great loss of life to storm it. The only way, in my opinion, is by a turning movement round the right of the enemy's position, for which I have not sufficient troops.'

This view I had also held, but seeing the very clever way in which Colonel Carthew-Yorstoun, of the Black Watch, was handling his battalion, I believed that after all he might gain the summit without great loss, though I hardly hoped that he would get off as easily as he actually did.

Like that of most of these table-mountains, the flat top of Babiaansberg was only accessible by a few kloofs, the greater part of its circumference being bounded by cliffs rising sheer for a hundred feet or so from the steep slope which formed its base. As nothing but one of the baboons after which the mountain was named could hope to reach the top by way of the cliffs, the Boers did not trouble to defend them, but gave all their attention to the kloofs. Towards the foot of a stretch of precipice Colonel Carthew-Yorstoun sent a couple of companies, which, keeping well away from the defended kloof, reached the top of the slope unobserved, and then, moving to their right along the 'dead ground' under the rocky wall, got into a position from which they could command the kloof. There they remained, well under cover, and reserving their fire, while the remainder of the battalion, taking the fullest advantage of ground, crept up the slope to their right. The slope was so steep, and the Highlanders so skilful, that for a time the Boers did not seem to know of their advance; but at last the alarm was given, and a warm fire opened on the advancing companies. But good shooting down a steep hill is always difficult, even when one has time to aim carefully, and this Grant and the companies on the left took care the enemy should not do. As soon as the Boers opened fire the Highlanders replied with a rattle of bullets among the stones of the kloof, into which the Naval guns also sent shell after shell in a way that must have been very upsetting to the marksmen's aim.

The result of the flank fire from the Highland companies was that the Boers simply could not show their heads above their 'scances,' and their fire was wild and harmless; that of Grant's shells, that they found the kloof was not good enough to stay in at all, and gradually slipped out of it on to the table-top. We could not see this at the time, and wasted a certain amount of lead and iron on harmless rocks, till the Highlanders got so near the kloof that Grant had to cease fire. Then, as they entered it, we saw the Boers on their ponies streaming across the plateau to the south-eastward, and knew that Babiaansberg was ours. This, however, was not known to the Black Watch, and the last part of their assault was none the less fine because it did not happen to be opposed. They knew the hill was strongly held, and could not tell what number of the enemy might be lying on the top ready to open a murderous fire on them from all sides as they came out of the ravine.

There is nothing so alarming as the unknown, and I am inclined to think that, although the whole assault only cost three men wounded, that dash up the dark chasm on to the doubtful tableland was as grand an act as even their advance across the plain of Paardeberg.

I have described this assault as I saw it, for Colonel Carthew-Yorstoun's report was brief, modest and business-like, but gave few details. If I have left out anything that I should have put in, I hope the Black Watch will forgive me.

When we had once gained the top, it became a regular trap for the Boers. The bulk of Hamilton's force was on their right, a few of his Mounted Infantry on their left, and before long he would have some in their rear. Realizing this, they galloped away before it was too late, and, beyond a few long-range shots in the earlier stage of their advance, neither the Highland Light Infantry nor the Seaforths were opposed. The Argyll and Sutherlands were in reserve.

Soon after this I had a message from Hamilton,

telling me that he had taken the ridge to the north of Babiaansberg, and was then going to attack a kopje about a mile and a half further north. He said that some of the enemy, apparently from Brandfort, were on his left flank, and that it would help him greatly if I would stop where I was till the road was clear for a convoy of 100 waggons which he was expecting. I therefore sent orders for the troops to concentrate at Susannafontein, a dam near the north-western angle of the mountain, and then sent a message to Hamilton telling him where we were, and that I would look after his convoy. At about half-past five I had a message from him which, after thanking me for my help in the fight, said: 'Converging columns are retiring in Winburg direction from here, Brandfort and Thaba 'Nchu. I hope to camp near Welkom; anticipate strong opposition at drift near Vet River to-morrow.'

This looked as if he might want our support again, but, not knowing what sort of country he had to get through, was doubtful whether this or bringing on the convoy was most urgent. Also we were only rationed up to that day, and anything like a long halt for the convoy would have reduced us nearly to starvation. I therefore sent him the following message :

'May 10th, 6.10 p.m. If convoy does not arrive in the night, would you prefer me to wait for it here, or to push on in your support? I have left my mounted troops near your late camp to look out for it, and rely on you to let me know if it reaches you by any other route. I am only supplied up to tomorrow night on half-rations, and if the convoy does not come, or I miss it, I hope you will be able to help me. I believe your 21st Brigade is rationed up to Sunday night,* and this neighbourhood having been cleared by your troops, I cannot get any local supplies.'

As we could not get heliographic communication with Hamilton, this was sent by an orderly, who lost his road in the dark; so, having got no answer by four next morning, I sent Nugent with a copy of it, and told him to see Hamilton and explain the situation, and also let me know how they stood near Welkom. When day broke the Eastern Province Horse reported that the convoy was in sight, and the country clear of the enemy, so I left an escort of them on the ridge above Verkerdes Vlei to bring it on, and started off after Hamilton. On the way we met Nugent, who reported that the troops ahead had met with no opposition, and were about to march for Winburg, and that Hamilton had kindly left me half a day's rations.

A march of about ten miles brought us to the Welkom Drift of the Vet River, on the further side of which Hamilton had bivouacked, and from which his rearguard was just moving off.

* This was written on Friday. The same information was sent to the Chief of the Staff.

Why, with such a position as this to defend, the Boers should have chosen the Babiaansberg one has always puzzled me. Marching across an open plain, we saw in front of us a line of low kopjes, which seemed to rise from its north-western edge. Neither trees nor houses were visible, nor any break in the plain to hint at the position of the river, which I thought must be beyond the kopjes. Gradually, however, the ground began to fall, getting steeper and steeper, till it became a glacis-like slope, from the foot of which sprung low, irregular masses of rock, rising as we neared them till they eclipsed the line of kopjes. But it was not until we were within 500 yards of these that we found that between them and us ran a ravine some 150 yards wide, in whose bed sheer below us flowed the Vet. A road had been cut obliquely down the steep western bank, and then, crossing the river, followed the bottom of the ravine for about three-quarters of a mile, out of which it gradually worked up on the other side, through very broken ground to the level of the plain.

I have rarely seen a place which I should have liked less to attack, or one which seemed more suited to Boer tactics. Of course, if we had had good maps and Intelligence reports, we should have known all about it, and probably have managed to take it; but, as things were, there would have been every chance of our marching right up to the ravine before we found it out, and getting the full benefit of the enemy's fire while we lay fully exposed on the plain. I do not think our scouts would ever have found it out, for, as I have said, the curious shape of the ground led one to believe that the river was on the further side of the kopjes till one got a great deal closer to it than they would have been allowed to do.

It was not only a good place to hold, but a bad one to retire over, and we heard that the Boers' retreat over it the day before had been anything but an orderly one, men, guns and waggons crowding together on the narrow road in hopeless confusion. They, however, all got safely across.

We bivouacked on the plain about two miles beyond the river, so as to get clear of the broken ground, after a short and easy march for the troops, but it was late in the afternoon before the last of the transport had crossed the drift.

At about half-past three I had a message from Hamilton, dated Winburg, enclosing a telegram from Lord Roberts, urging him to push on as fast as possible. He said he was only rationed up to the following night, would have to make a forced march next day, and that it was of the utmost importance that his convoy should reach him in the morning. He therefore asked me to load up my transport with supplies from his convoy as soon as it arrived, and send it straight on to Winburg.

My latest news of the convoy was that it was outspanned about twelve miles back, but was going to inspan again at four. Knowing the difficulties of the drift, I had no hope of its reaching us in less than eight hours; but I sent an order back to the officer commanding it to push on with all speed, and not to halt till he overtook us. There was the further difficulty, in carrying out Hamilton's wishes, that his force being more than three times as large as mine,* the whole of my transport was insufficient to give him more than temporary help; and as he was going to make forced marches from Winburg, it seemed likely that, if he started without his convoy, it would never catch him up. Also, if we sent him what we could, we should either have to transfer the loads of the first waggons that came in to our mule-waggons, and risk sending him nothing but forage, or biscuits, or whatever these might be loaded with, or else wait till the last waggon was in, and spend several hours in sorting all the packages in the dark. As I did not see how in any case it could be very satisfactory, I thought he had better decide for himself what he would like done, and sent the following:

'Convoy cannot reach here before midnight. Restarting at 4 a.m., it may reach Winburg at noon if oxen do not break down. Can send 150,000 pounds by my mule transport, to reach Winburg by 9 a.m. If you wish this quantity hastened, say how you wish it made up.'

* It consisted of the Mounted Infantry Division, the Second Cavalry Brigade, the Nineteenth and Twenty-first Infantry Brigades, and six batteries.

To this he answered :

' As choice of evils, I think I had better wait for convoy, and then make a march which will run on into the night.'

The convoy dribbled in during the night, and was pushed on again as fast as possible ; but between us and Winburg was the Klein Vet River, running, like all these streams, between high sandy banks, which caused much delay, and it was past one next day before the last of the waggons reached Winburg, and about four in the afternoon before Hamilton was able to march. As it turned out, there had been no need for all this hurry, for a couple of hours after he had gone I received a telegram from Lord Roberts saying that if Hamilton had left, I was to send a special messenger after him, telling him to halt till further orders, as the Commander-in-Chief was obliged to wait at Smaldeel for supplies.

CHAPTER VII

WINBURG

We reached Winburg at about noon on the 6th May. As Hamilton's troops covered so much ground, we could not settle down into a permanent bivouac; but having chosen the best temporary place I could find for mine, I went to see Hamilton, whom I found in the Landdrost's office, busy writing his despatch on his engagement of the 4th.

As I did not then know what the intentions at Headquarters might be as to my future movements, I thought it best to discuss our relative positions frankly with him. These were very unusual. I was a Major-General and local Lieutenant-General, nominally commanding a division, and still officially addressed by Headquarters as G.O.C. Ninth Division. But my force consisted of only one infantry brigade, a handful of cavalry, and two naval guns. Hamilton, a Colonel and local Major-General,[*] was

---

[*] In a later edition of the Army List the date of his local rank is given as the 10th April, 1900, but in the list issued by Headquarters at Bloemfontein on the 29th April, 1900, he was shown as Colonel and local Major-General.

in command of a much larger force, of which one of my brigades formed part.* He had received orders from the Commander-in-Chief, of which I was ignorant, and a message from the Chief of the Staff, informing him what troops would be under his command, and giving him the orders for my division. A copy of this message had been sent to me, and I had been told to comply with the orders in it. These were to march a certain distance in rear of Hamilton, and be prepared to support him 'if required.' As long as this support was not required, the position, although unusual, offered no special difficulties. An army does not march in the order of the seniority of its Generals, and if the Commander-in-Chief thought it best that we should be in reserve, there was nothing more to be said.

But from the moment Hamilton felt that he wanted my help the possibility of endless complications arose. He as junior could neither order me up nor dispose my troops, while Lord Roberts' evident intention that he should direct practically prevented me from taking command. Neither of us made difficulties, and, thanks to Hamilton's tact, everything worked smoothly; but it struck me that if it were intended that the Highland Brigade should remain in reserve to Hamilton's column, there would

* I was never informed that the Nineteenth Brigade had ceased to form part of my division, and in the list of the 29th April, above mentioned, it and the 83rd, 84th and 85th Batteries were shown as belonging to it.

be less risk of hitches if it were simply under command of its own Brigadier, who was Hamilton's junior, and as such would be completely under his orders. After talking all this over with Hamilton, and telling him what I proposed to say, I telegraphed to the Chief of the Staff, suggesting that, if the Highland Brigade was to follow Hamilton's column any further, it would be better that it should do so under Macdonald, and that I and the Divisional Staff should remain at Winburg. I then explained the situation more fully in the following letter to the Military Secretary :

'WINBURG,
'6.5.00.

' DEAR COWAN,

' Re my telegram to the C. of S. this morning, I hope the Chief does not think either that there has been any friction or that I am troubling about my dignity. Thanks to Hamilton, nothing could have been more pleasant (personally) than our relations ; but that does not alter the fact that the situation has been an awkward one for both of us. Feeling sure from Lord Roberts' telegram that he wished Hamilton to command, I have done my best to fall in with his wishes, and I hope I have succeeded in doing all that Hamilton wished ; but the fact of his not being able to give me actual orders must rather have hampered him, while his tactfulness in refraining from too direct a statement of his wishes forced me to have to guess at them. Having nothing to do but fall in with his movements and views, I had nothing actually to complain of; but I cannot help feeling that on an occasion like the engagement of the 4th nothing could absolve me from the responsibility of senior officer, and had anything gone wrong, I alone should have had to take the blame. As it is, Hamilton will very rightly get the credit for his well-planned and successful engagement; but, in justice to myself, I hope the Chief will not mind my pointing out that for Hamilton it was a case of "Heads I win, tails you lose." All the same, I should not have telegraphed as I did this morning had not Hamilton previously agreed with me that it would be more satisfactory if the situation was cleared up.

'Yours sincerely,
'H. E. COLVILE.'

I received no answer to this letter, but in the evening had a telegram from the Chief of the Staff, answering mine of that morning, and also that of the 4th, in which I had told him that our half-rations would be exhausted on the 5th. It said:

'You will have to garrison Winburg when Ian Hamilton goes on, and, as it is impossible to send you supplies, you must supply yourself from country. Make the people bake bread, and collect live stock for your wants. Do what you can to repair telegraph line between us; we will also send out from here.'

I was still thinking over this ingenious solution of the ever-present supply problem, when I received the following telegram from Hamilton :

'My Supply officer handed over to Captain Piggott the papers showing supplies available in Winburg. I had strict injunctions to requisition everything I could carry, and this was done; but now I have been halted, I can take another day's supplies — namely, 30,000 pounds mealies, 2,500 pounds sugar, 13,000 pounds flour, 400 pounds salt, and all available tea. I am holding my wagons in readiness to send for this stuff. Kindly wire quickly if you can let me have it, and if you can spare fatigue party to load it up. I shall await your reply before starting off wagons.'

Charity, we are told, covers a multitude of sins; but it also begins at home, and whatever the number of my iniquities may have been, I know that of my men was 4,000—all hungry.

Winburg was a pretty village with a good deal of market-square and church and a sprinkling of houses. Out of it, Hamilton had just taken 'everything' he could 'carry' for his 11,000 men and 12,000 animals, and into it I had just marched with my rations exhausted, and with about fifty mounted men to help me supply myself 'from the country,' and in which, by the Chief of the Staff's 'Circular Memorandum' of 'Instructions for Officers Commanding Posts in the Orange Free State,' I was told that 'reserves of food and forage must never be allowed to fall below 60 days for the entire garrison.'* I hope, therefore, that I may be forgiven for telling Hamilton firmly, but I hope gently, that I could not grant his last request.

Ewart and Humphreys had both felt so ill at Welkom Drift that Dorman had ordered them to do the last march in a Cape cart; and on reaching Winburg they were sent to bed, having the high temperature and usual symptoms of the prevalent fever, which either passed off in about ten days or developed into enteric. Ewart's took the former, and Humphreys' the latter course, and we never saw him again; his place was taken by Pigott, the Highland Brigade Supply officer, and a better one I never hope to meet. Ewart's place was temporarily taken by Cuthbertson, our Deputy-Assistant-Adjutant-General.

As soon as he had occupied the town, Hamilton had offered the post of Landdrost to Mr. Van Zyl, a leading inhabitant, but that gentleman had reserved his answer. On the 7th, however, he wrote to say he accepted the position, and I saw him next morning, and, after explaining what we expected of him, duly appointed him. Next day Lieutenant Cloete, of Roberts' Horse, arrived, and handed me the following telegram:

* From the 23rd April to the 28th June, when the division was broken up, I never had more than ten days' rations in hand, and rarely more than four.

'TO GENL. IAN HAMILTON, CABLE CART, VIÂ WINBURG.

'8th May.—Please send Cloete, of Roberts' Horse, to Winburg to take up Landdrost duties.—M. S., Chief.'

As this was all the information in the hands of either Cloete or myself, I telegraphed to the Military Secretary that I had confirmed Hamilton's appointment of Van Zyl, and asked for instructions. In answer I was told, 'No one has power to appoint Landdrost except Chief. Cloete should take up duties.' So I had to let Mr. Van Zyl know that the bargain was off.

Nothing of any importance happened for the next few days, which were spent in strengthening the position, repairing the railway, trying (with a good deal of success) to get the neighbouring farmers to come in and lay down their arms, and in collecting supplies.

Our first excitement was caused by the arrival on the 12th of a convoy from the railway of eleven waggons with supplies, and at noon on the 15th the first train steamed in, bringing more supplies and our mails. On the same day I had a telegram from the Military Secretary, asking me to expedite my reply to an extract from Broadwood's despatch which he had sent me on the 25th April. I had not received this, and answered to that effect; but next day it came by train. It had been addressed to me at the Waterworks, which I had not left till the morning of the 30th, so it should have reached me there.

The extract in question was the now well-known paragraph 9, and ran as follows:

'About noon a Staff officer arrived from the G.O.C. 9th Division to say he had reached Boesman's Kop. I suggested that a direct advance on the Spruit offered the best chance of assisting. About 2 p.m. I was informed that the 9th Division had moved towards Watervaal Drift; so, seeing any hope of recapturing the guns at an end, I began sending the units to their camps, the Mounted Infantry and guns to Bloemfontein, and the cavalry to Springfield, as, owing to the loss of the baggage, it was inadvisable to bivouac where we were.'

The Military Secretary said this was forwarded for any remarks I wished to make, more particularly as regards my reasons for not advancing from Boesman's Kop to the assistance of the cavalry brigade. As the correspondence on this subject has been already published, I will not interrupt the story by repeating it here, but those who wish to read it again can do so in Appendix II.

This was the hint to which I have already alluded, as to the mystery of my position during the last few weeks. Whether Lord Roberts agreed with Broad-wood that all chance of recapturing the guns was at an end when I marched on Waterval Drift, I, of course, did not know; but the allusion to my not advancing to the assistance of the cavalry showed that he was evidently under the impression that they had still required assistance. I own that my late position had rather depressed me; I could not understand what was the meaning of it, and although Hamilton had suggested that it was only due to accident, I could not agree. This correspondence, however, threw new light on it, and it seemed only necessary to let Lord Roberts know the facts of the case to put everything right.

Headquarters were then at Kroonstad, and we were daily expecting to hear of a forward movement, so the sooner my explanation went in, the better. I therefore told my Aide-de-Camp to see that an orderly with a good horse was ready to take my letter to Smaldeel, and set to work to write my answer as hard as I could.

While I was doing this, I was asked to issue the orders for a patrol of Eastern Province Horse, which was going towards Senekal. I was sending this patrol as the farmers who had come in said that many more would do so with a little encouragement; and as the road was reported by the Intelligence Department clear of the enemy, it seemed a good chance of giving it to them. There was nothing exceptional about the patrol, but I knew that the officer who was to command it was a thoroughly reliable one; and as I was writing against time, and full of my answer to Broadwood's despatch, I contented myself with verbally sketching the orders I wished given, and thought no more about it till, two days afterwards, we heard from native sources that thirteen Englishmen who had been seen going towards Senekal with a white flag had been made prisoners. As these were evidently those of my patrol, I telegraphed to the Chief of the Staff, explaining how and why one had been sent, and saying that I was afraid the men had been treacherously made prisoners at Senekal. He answered: 'The Commander-in-Chief regrets the capture of this party, and considers that it was most injudicious to send a patrol of twenty men to any great distance from the Head Quarters when the enemy was known to be moving about.'

In the meanwhile I had learnt that, not having twenty sound horses free, the officer temporarily* commanding the Eastern Province Horse had only sent a patrol of twelve. The Intelligence Department having also got some details of the capture, which was evidently treacherous, I sent a written report to the Chief of the Staff, saying that the Intelligence agents had reported the road clear as far as they had been—*i.e.*, about twenty-five miles; that the bulk of the Boers, who were retreating before the Eighth Division, appeared to be near Korunna Pass—*i.e.*, about forty miles S.S.W. of Senekal; and that Senekal was practically empty.

That burghers who had come in stated that a

* The commanding officer was ill.

number of others would do so if they were assured that they would not be made prisoners.

That I had sent the patrol under a white flag, with orders to invite burghers to come in, but, as it might meet small parties of Boers who would not respect the white flag, I thought it best to make it fairly strong, and had fixed the strength at twenty.

That the officer commanding had orders not to send more than two men into the town, and these under a white flag, and then only if the town was not in possession of a commando.

That he was to remember that he was on a peaceful mission, and was to retire at once if there seemed to be any chance of opposition.

That the whole party under a white flag was reported to have been made prisoners five miles to the south-west of Senekal without a shot being fired.

The consequences of this capture were not very disastrous, as Lieutenant Bowker and his twelve men came back in due course safe and sound, and did not even lose their kits, which had not yet been forwarded from Bloemfontein. As I heard no more about it from Headquarters, I may have been absolved ; but as it is the only one for which I accept the responsibility, I have described it at some length, that it may be entered, at whatever its value may be, in the bad side of my account.

On the 17th the Chief of the Staff telegraphed :

' Send Macdonald and two battalions by march

route to Ventersburg. Two howitzers should accompany the column. ... He should go to-night if possible.'

I sent off Macdonald that evening, as ordered, with the Black Watch and Argyll and Sutherland Highlanders. As the supplies he was to take were not mentioned, I gave him four days' rations, which was as much as he could carry, and also sent with him a section of the Divisional Engineer Company with pumps for water-supply. As the Howitzer Battery had been left at the Waterworks on the 29th April by order of the Chief of the Staff, I could not comply with the part of his telegram relating to that.

This reduced my command to the Seaforth Highlanders, the Highland Light Infantry, the detachments of Eastern Province Horse and Naval Brigade, and half the 7th Company Royal Engineers.[*] But, having reached its lowest ebb (for the moment), the tide began to show signs of turning.

On the following day I had telegrams from the Assistant-Adjutant-General at Headquarters, telling me that we were to come on to Kroonstad as soon as relief could arrive from Bloemfontein; from the Military Secretary, giving the position and movements of the various columns, from Hunter's in the west to Hamilton's in the east; and from the chief Staff officer at Bloemfontein, informing me that the Twelfth Brigade had been ordered to Winburg.

[*] I had given Smith-Dorrien one section.

The leading companies of the Bedfordshire Regiment arrived by train early next morning, and on hearing this from me the Chief of the Staff telegraphed from Kroonstad :

'Now that Twelfth Brigade has commenced to arrive, the remainder of the Ninth Division will march to Ventersburg, whence your command will move on Lindley under further orders, which will be sent you. You should arrange for supplies for this march from Winburg. The fifth Battery R.F.A. has been ordered to be railed to Winburg to accompany you, and you should await its arrival before marching. The Field Hospital, Highland Brigade, and the Detachment, 62 all ranks, E.P. Horse, have been ordered to march from here to Ventersburg, starting to-morrow morning; these should arrive twenty-first at Ventersburg. The Thirteenth Battalion of Yeomanry from Bloemfontein has been ordered to join you at Ventersburg, and you will receive further information as to the date of its arrival there.'

On the 20th, in answer to an inquiry from me, the Chief of the Staff telegraphed that the naval guns should accompany me, and gave me the further welcome news that the whole of the kits of the Eastern Province Horse had been sent to Ventersburg, but he added: 'Only two Companies of Thirteenth Battalion Yeomanry, and possibly one Mounted Company Lovat's Corps, will be able to join you at Ventersburg by the twenty-third, but the other two Yeomanry Companies will follow as soon as possible.'

Later on the same day I received from the Chief of the Staff the 'further orders' promised in the telegram of the 19th. The message was headed, 'Clear the line,'* and ran as follows :

'From Ventersburg the Highland Brigade march to Lindley, and thence to Heilbron. Regarding supplies, D. of S. will communicate with you on subject. Take as much as you can from Winburg. Brigade will be concentrated Ventersburg twenty-third, reach Lindley twenty-sixth, and Heilbron twenty-ninth.'

This was the last telegram which I received from the Chief of the Staff until after I had reached Heilbron ; it was also the only one of the series which had been sent in cipher. As the only fresh information it gave me was on the destination of the column and the dates on which it was to reach the various stages of its advance, it was evident that these were parts of my orders which were considered secret and specially important. The telegram itself did not give much information as to the part which the Ninth Division was to play, but from the Military Secretary's telegram of the 18th I knew the position of the various columns, which were

* An instruction for the telegraph staff prefixed to pressing messages, which gave them precedence of all others.

echeloned across the Free State, with the left forward on the Vaal. From a mass of telegrams on supply and transport matters, it was evident that a forward movement of the whole army was in hand, while, from the sudden increase of my command by a battery of artillery and some 500 or 600 cavalry, it seemed as if the Highland Brigade was at last to be relieved from what Macdonald had called 'the rôle of rearguard.'

Rundle's and Brabant's waggons were then waiting at Winburg for the trains bringing their supplies, and the former had telegraphed that he only wanted these to enable him to push northwards. Lindley, I knew, was in our hands, and had been taken by a force moving from Kroonstad; and as we were ordered to take the rather roundabout way to it viâ Lindley, instead of following the direct Senekal road, it seemed likely that we were intended to sweep the country immediately to the east of the railway, while Rundle and Brabant would look after the extreme right, viâ Senekal, Bethlehem, Reitz, and Vrede, and join hands with the Natal Army. If so, Heilbron (at the head of a branch line of railway) would become their supply depot, as Winburg then was.

A definite date (the 29th of May) was fixed for our arrival at Heilbron, to keep up to which we should have to make forced marches all the way. From the fact that this was the only part of my orders which it had been thought necessary to send in cipher, it was evident that some important movement was intended to take place on that day, which would probably include the seizure of Wolvehoek Junction* by the central column.

Three days after the receipt of these orders, I learnt that Heilbron had been occupied by Hamilton, and as Headquarters and the Seventh and Eleventh Divisions were still at Kroonstad, this pointed to a dash ahead by the Mounted Infantry Division to seize a strategic position (and possibly some rolling stock), which it would hold till it was set free by our arrival. I do not know whether this was contemplated when my orders were framed, so cannot tell whether my original guess at the 'general idea' was wrong or not; but while it somewhat modified my conception of it, it made the necessity for our forced march to Heilbron more clear.

At the moment chosen for the advance on the Vaal, it was obviously important that no part of a mobile force such as the Mounted Infantry Division should be detained for garrison duty, and it was evidently our business to relieve it. But the addition of cavalry and artillery which had just been made to my force raised hopes that we too were destined to take part in the general advance of the army, and that, with the railway to Heilbron open, we should in our turn soon be relieved by Line of Communication troops.

* The junction of the Main and Heilbron lines.

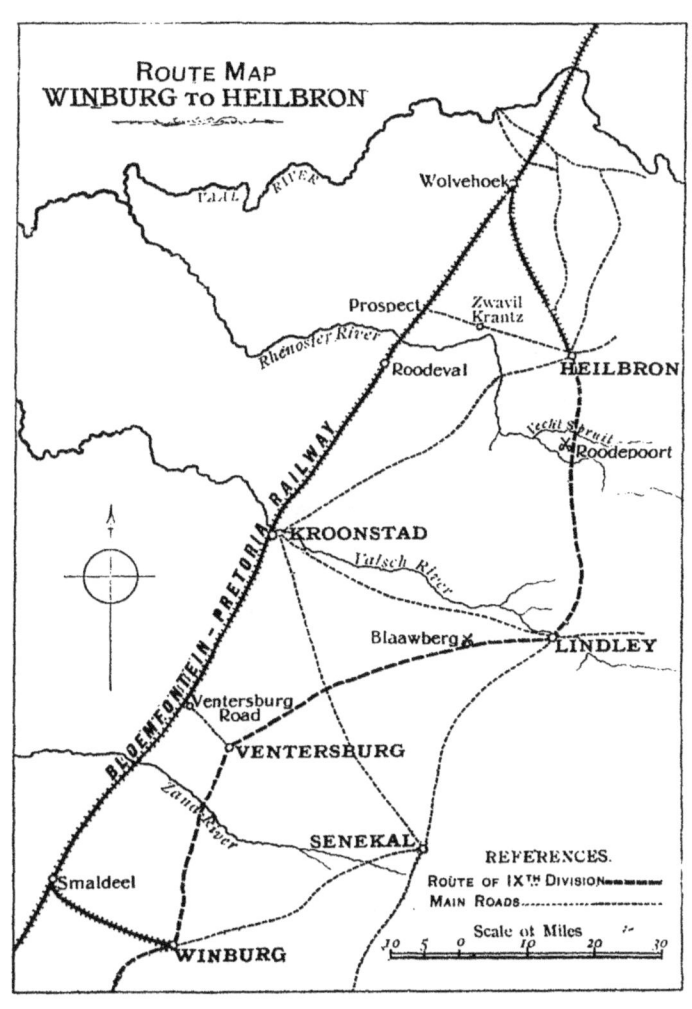

In the meanwhile, there was plenty to speculate about as to our more immediate future, these speculations being chiefly on the eternal supply question. Macdonald, as I have said, had marched to Ventersburg on the 17th with four days' supplies, and, as I had not been told whether I was to ration him from Winburg or whether he would be supplied direct by Headquarters, I telegraphed on the 15th to the Director of Supplies, asking how Macdonald's force was to be fed after the 21st, and also letting him know how we stood.* Getting no answer to this, I repeated the question to the Chief of the Staff on the 19th, adding that I could only carry four days' supplies, and asking him to arrange for their despatch to meet me at Ventersburg from the railway, and that unless this was done Macdonald would be without supplies by the time I reached him. The only information I got in reply was that in his telegram of the same date quoted above, telling me that the Director of Supplies would communicate with me.

In the meanwhile, Kelly-Kenny had telegraphed from Bloemfontein to ask what supplies his Twelfth Brigade would find at Winburg, and Rundle's and Brabant's waggons were waiting to take those for the Eighth and Colonial Divisions; so I again telegraphed to the Director of Supplies, saying that, if all these demands were to be met, additional supplies must be sent at once, and reminded him

* We had then eight days' supplies of most things for 3,000 men.

that I had no instructions as to how Macdonald was to be rationed.

The answer to this was received on the 20th as follows :

'Instructions have been issued for a reserve of 14 days for 2,000 men, 1,500 horses, and 3,000 mules, to be maintained at Winburg, and sent there at once by train. This is for your own troops, Eighth Division, and Colonial Division. Quartermaster Bradshaw should assume charge of this depot. Am sending seven days' forage and supplies from Zand River and Ventersburg for Battalions of Highland Brigade. After this reserve is completed, troops at Ventersburg should draw from Zand River with their own transport to maintain this reserve. The convoy will leave Zand River on the 21st for Ventersburg. It should be guarded by an escort, which you should arrange with Comnt. Zand River.'

This was satisfactory as far as it went. We were to have plentiful supplies at Winburg—when they arrived ; we should have seven days' rations at Ventersburg with which to start on our march to Heilbron, if we could fetch them to and carry them from that place. But the supplies had not arrived at Winburg, and the carrying power of Macdonald's transport was only four days' rations for his force, and therefore little over one and a quarter days* for

* Accurately 1·273.

the whole column which had to be rationed. As his mules could not do the twenty-miles return journey from Ventersburg to Zand River* more than once a day, it would take him about five and a half days to carry the seven days' reserve it was required to complete at Ventersburg in three days, even if his force did not draw on it, which of course it would have to do. It is true plentiful supplies were promised for Winburg; but even if they came, the carrying power of my transport was no greater than that of Macdonald's, and, deducting the two days' rations we should eat on the road, I should be able to contribute less than three-quarters of a day's supplies for the whole force.

So much for our chance of getting food; but there was the further complication that, even if we did get it, the divisional transport would only carry two and a half days' rations for the increased force, while our march to Heilbron was timed by the Chief of the Staff to last for six days.†

On receipt of this message, I telegraphed to the Commandant at Zand River, asking what escort he could provide, and got an answer that one officer and ten men were the most he could raise. I also sent the following to the Director of Supplies:

'No supplies have arrived here as yet by train either for Rundle, Brabant, or myself. I am ordered to march north as soon as joined by a battery of

* The bridge having been destroyed, this was then 'Rail head.'
† Including the days of arrival and departure.

Field Artillery, and have five days' supplies from tomorrow for my force, which consists of 2 Battalions, Divisional details, Artillery and Naval Brigade. I can only carry 4 days' supplies from here, and should like to replenish at Ventersburg, where I shall be joined by Macdonald with two more Battalions and by 4 companies Imperial Yeomanry. Macdonald is rationed up to 21st. The total strength of my force at Ventersburg, from which place I move eastward, will then be 5,500 men, 1,000 horses, and 1,000 mules. I cannot possibly leave Quartermaster Bradshaw here, as he is the only Supply officer with me, Pigott being at Ventersburg. I cannot get any transport locally, and have only Divisional mule Transport.'

In answer to this, the Director of Supplies telegraphed:

'Have wired inquiring why rations have not reached Winburg, and directing them to be hastened. Am arranging for 3,300 rations biscuit, 3,000 rations preserved meat, 4,400 rations groceries, and 6,000 rations forage. Portion of this will be conveyed in ox-wagons to Ventersburg to-morrow morning from Zand River. 3rd Brigade has been instructed to send all their mule-wagons to Zand River also to-morrow morning to draw remainder. Such ox-wagons as are required to convey supplies will accompany your column on march; remainder will rejoin supply party viâ

Kroonstadt when empty. Captain Terry ordered to proceed Winburg at once in A.S.C. charge. Lieut. and Quartermaster Bradshaw will accompany you.'

This promised us six days' rations of biscuit, eight days of groceries, half a day of preserved meat, and three days' forage—*i.e.*, just enough biscuit (by far the most important item) to take us to Heilbron, and further gave me a free hand to take as much ox transport as I required to carry it; but the statement that only a 'portion of this will be conveyed in ox-wagons to Ventersburg,' and that the Third Brigade (*i.e.*, Highlanders) had been instructed to send their mule-wagons ... to draw the remainder,' left some doubt in my mind as to whether the Director of Supplies realized that Macdonald only had half the brigade transport with him. It also only provided forage for half our march. I therefore telegraphed on the 21st:

'Only two Battalions Highland Brigade are at Ventersburg and available to send mule-wagons to fetch supplies from Zand River to meet me at Ventersburg. I note that you are only sending 3 days' forage for me to Ventersburg.'

I also told him that Rundle's and Brabant's waggons were waiting for supplies, which had not yet arrived.

In answer to this, the Director of Supplies wired the same day:

'Have ordered ten additional ox-wagons to proceed from Zand River to Ventersburg. Have directed G.O.C. there to send ten mule-wagons to convey supplies from Zand River. Have already wired railway authorities to send on supplies, and am repeating wire urgently.'

This at last seemed to settle the question of our supplies, and I went to sleep that night in the hope that for once in a way the Highland Brigade would be able to do a march on full rations; for, of course, I assumed that the Director of Supplies at Headquarters was in the confidence of the Commander-in-Chief and Chief of the Staff, and that, as he had limited us to the exact amount which would take us to Heilbron, he knew that we should be able to replenish there.

As I left next morning, I never heard how the columns to the east got on; but my last telegram to the Director of Supplies said:

'A train with forage and biscuits has arrived for Rundle and Brabant, but no groceries, for which they press urgently. 38 wagons have arrived here from Brabant for supplies.'

Before all these rather intricate supply questions arose, Ewart was off the sick-list, and by his forethought and businesslike methods was of the greatest help to me; but Humphreys, whose special department it was, was still ill, and Pigott, who had temporarily taken his place, had gone to Ventersburg with Macdonald. Luckily, Long was still with us, as keen as ever to do his best, and he unselfishly took much of the work off Ewart's and Cuthbertson's hands.

As Ewart recovered, my two Aides-de-Camp, Nugent and Campbell, fell ill with the same feverish symptoms, which with both turned into enteric. Nugent was sent to Bloemfontein, and I left Campbell in hospital at Winburg, taking my 'galloper,' Murray, on with me, and telegraphing for Captain McLeod, of the West Riding Regiment, as temporary Aide-de-Camp; but he could not reach me before we marched, and on his way after us got enteric and was taken prisoner.

I had been ordered to march as soon as the battery arrived; and as I had heard on the 18th that arrangements had been made for its being sent up by train, I hoped to get off, at latest, on the morning of the 21st. On the 20th I heard that it had passed Vet River, and telegraphed to the various Commandants to let me know when it reached their stations; but after waiting all day and night, and hearing nothing, the first half of it steamed in without warning on the morning of the 21st. Major Lane, who commanded it, believed that the remaining two guns were not far behind; but it was four in the afternoon before they arrived, and I thought it better to let the horses rest for a night after their railway journey, and issued orders for our start to be at daylight next morning.

A truck full of clothing, for which we had long been waiting, failed to reach us before we left, so the men had again to march in their rags, and the battery had no ammunition column with it; but with these exceptions (if everything promised turned up at Ventersburg) we were fairly complete, and seemed likely to make a fairer start than we had yet had a chance of doing.

CHAPTER VIII

WINBURG TO LINDLEY

ON the morning of the 22nd May I handed over the command at Winburg to General Clements, commanding the Twelfth Brigade, and at six we marched off. The weather had got much cooler, and the men, who thought we were going to Kroonstad, were in the best of spirits at the prospect of getting to the front again, and stepped out well. At four in the afternoon we reached Mr. Tennant's store at the Zand River Drift, nineteen miles from Winburg, and bivouacked. There I had a memorandum from Macdonald pointing out that by branching off to the right four miles short of Ventersburg, and bivouacking at Roode Kraal, we should cut off a corner and save the men about five miles. This seemed a very good suggestion, but the only drawback to it was that it would show the direction in which we intended to march, so I answered that before deciding on it I would come on to Ventersburg myself.

Next morning early I galloped on, leaving Colonel Hughes-Hallett in command of the column, with orders what to do if he received a message from me to branch off at Goede Hoep. Reaching Ventersburg at half-past eight, I learnt from Macdonald that our destination was common knowledge in the camp (and consequently in the town), so sent back a message to Hughes-Hallett to march on Roode Kraal.

Macdonald also said that he had sent his Aide-de-Camp, Captain Wigham, into Kroonstad the day before to make a personal appeal at Headquarters on the subject of transport, and that he had been told by the Headquarter Staff that there was no chance of the Yeomanry arriving in time. This was annoying, as, although the drafts of the Eastern Province Horse which had arrived brought my mounted troops up to 107 of all ranks, this was not enough for scouting and protecting some three miles of guns and waggons.*

* Counting a mule waggon with 10 mules at 32 yards, an ox-waggon with 16 oxen at 40 yards, a Naval gun with 32 oxen at 80 yards, the length of our column, without infantry or cavalry, was approximately as follows, when closed up:

	Yards.
Battery with waggons	240
First Line Transport, including Naval guns, R.E., etc.	1,580
Second Line Transport	2,471
Ox convoy	840
Mess and brigade carts, etc.	375
	5,506
'Tailing' would probably increase this by about	1,000
Total	6,506 = about 3¾ miles.

WINBURG TO LINDLEY 159

There were various surmises as to what had become of the Yeomanry, and where they would go to; but if they did not turn up in the next twenty-four hours it was certain that we should not see them, at any rate, till we reached Heilbron. I own that I had some doubts (which were justified, though not in the way I expected) whether I should see them at all, for I was getting accustomed to troops being given and taken away, and thought it quite likely that some other use had been found for them. However, I said nothing about this, but telegraphed to the Chief of the Staff reporting the arrival of the other troops and Divisional Staff, and that there were no signs of the Yeomanry.

Although the Field Hospital had at last joined us, we were still very short of medical officers, having only seven, besides the P.M.O., while some units had none at all. This I also reported to the Chief of the Staff.

Macdonald and his two battalions marched after the men's dinner to Roode Kraal, to join Hughes-Hallett, but I stayed in Ventersburg with my Staff and the telegraph clerks, to be near the office in case any message came. It was a dreary, deserted-looking place, without any of the pretty, well-to-do look of most Free State villages; its only redeeming feature was an old gentleman who said he had been persecuted by the Transvaal Government, and drove up and down the single street waving a

Union Jack and throwing money to the troops as they marched out.

I reached the bivouac next morning before the brigade marched off, and for a moment wondered whether I had got into the wrong camp. For instead of the helmeted heads to which I was accustomed I saw nothing but a mass of 'dopper' hats. I had talked over the question of head-dress with Macdonald at Bloemfontein, and had said that if he could get leave from Headquarters, as he suggested, I was all in favour of the soft felt hats being issued in place of his worn-out helmets.

This conversation had taken place early in March, and I had thought no more about it; but it seemed that during his stay at Ventersburg he had managed to get hold of the hats, but had not issued them till the whole brigade was concentrated. The mixture of the kilt and slouch hat ('Boer above and bare below,' as somebody put it) was at first sight rather startling, the more so that the men wore them in that shamefaced sort of way peculiar to the Britisher in fancy dress. They soon got accustomed to them, however, and each regiment invented some knowing-looking little feather or badge with which to ornament one side, and we got to look upon them as being as smart as they were undoubtedly comfortable and convenient.

We marched about eighteen miles to Blaauwbosch Bank, a farm on the Senekal-Kroonstad road, where we learnt from the proprietor that we were likely to meet with opposition before reaching Lindley. As this was the Queen's Birthday, I ordered a ration of rum to be served out to the troops; but there was not quite enough to go round, and the Divisional Staff had to do without, so that my servant did not know the reason of the cheering with which it was drunk, and came up to me in a great state of excitement to ask if I would tell him what the victory was.

Anything more dreary than the burnt-up veldt at this time of year it is difficult to imagine: the sky-line in front always cut by a brown ridge exactly like the one that had just been passed, with, perhaps every ten miles, a clump of trees by a farm house, had so far made the marches seem very long and tedious; but although the character of the country did not change, the monotony of the marches came to an end by the middle of that day.

Soon after noon we reached the western side of a broad valley, running straight to the south, but curving away from us to the north-east. I was then with the main body, but, hearing a few shots ahead, rode on to the advance-guard, which had just crossed the level top of the ridge, and was beginning to descend into the valley. As I overtook it, I was handed a memorandum from the officer commanding the scouts of the Eastern Province Horse, saying that he had been fired at by a party of some 400 of the enemy from a farm-house, which we could see flying the usual white flag,* on the opposite side of the valley. I could not tell whether these 400 men were merely a small commando or part of a larger force; if the latter proved to be the case, I did not wish to commit myself and the whole force to a frontal attack on such a strong position as the opposite ridge appeared to be. I therefore told Macdonald to let the advanced guard feel its way carefully up the eastern slope to find out what was ahead of us, and halted the main body, which had not yet come up, and was still out of sight of the opposite crest. As the farmhouse was within range of the Naval guns, I brought them up ready to shell the position if the advanced guard was opposed.

Macdonald went on with the advanced guard, which I watched through my glasses till it had passed the farm and disappeared over the sky-line. Then, seeing that we should not have to fight for the ridge, I ordered the main body to advance. I learnt afterwards that Macdonald had sent a signal message, saying that the enemy had retired, but, as our signallers had then moved into the valley, it did not reach me. On topping the ridge we could see no signs of the advanced guard; I had, however, told Macdonald that I should halt at the first water

* As it was impossible to prevent small bodies of Boers from using the shelter afforded by farm buildings. President Steyn soon after this ordered all these white flags to be hauled down, as he very rightly thought that they only led to innocent farmers being held responsible for acts of treachery, or ones which appeared to be such.

we came to after noon, so I supposed that the cavalry had reported a good dam a short distance ahead, and that, finding the country clear of the enemy, he had pushed on to get his men into bivouac early. I, however, sent on a Staff Officer, who came back in about three-quarters of an hour with the report that he had reached a farm with excellent water, but had failed to see or hear anything of the advanced guard.

We were then on a fair road, not marked on the map, on the northern slope of the Maquaastadt, and leading to the nearest point of a cross-road, which was shown on the map as running into Lindley; but the guide said that there was another road round the southern slope which branched off from the one we were on at Maquaastadt Farm, and rejoined it near Spitz Kop (about four miles ahead). It was evident that the advanced guard had taken the southern road, so I sent a message to Macdonald that, as he had not left any connecting files, we had followed the northern and better road, and should halt at the first good water we came to after two o'clock.

At 2.45 we reached Mr. Jolliman's farm at Hopefield, and, learning that the junction of the roads was only about two miles to the E.S.E., I settled to halt there and send supplies on to the leading battalion. Half an hour afterwards, however, I had a message from Macdonald saying that the enemy, whose strength he could not tell, was occupying the surrounding hills, and asking for a battalion and some guns, as he could not encamp until they were cleared.

I therefore sent on the Black Watch and the Field Battery, but the enemy had retired before these reinforcements reached Macdonald. In trying to find out the strength of the enemy, Lieutenant Bertram, of the Eastern Province Horse, had unfortunately been wounded and taken prisoner; and there had been six other casualties, four of which were in the Eastern Province Horse, who also lost six horses. This incident was an example of the awkwardness of two Generals commanding one brigade. Had Macdonald been alone, he would have felt himself wholly responsible for the main body, and have either stayed with it himself or sent back such orders to it as he thought best; being only in command of the Highland Brigade, he had nothing to do with the divisional troops, but he could not bring up his three main body battalions without either leaving the artillery in the lurch or forcing me to move it whether I thought fit or not. Had we been a complete division, the cavalry would have been strong enough* to do all the work which fell to the Highland Brigade advanced guard, and Macdonald would simply have had orders to take his brigade in a certain direction for a certain purpose, making such internal arrangements as he thought best, while I should have had a second brigade in hand to use as the situation developed.

* Of my 107 mounted men, 33 were guarding the ox convoy and 20 scouting on each flank. Twelve horses were sick, but these were with the convoy guard.

As things were, at certain critical moments there was logically no middle course between my giving up the command of the division or Macdonald giving up that of the Highland Brigade, but practically neither of these could be done. Even if he had wished it, it was no more in my power to change his position than it was to escape the responsibilities of my own. The result was a compromise—generally an unsatisfactory way out of a difficulty—and it is remarkable that this was the only time that it did not work. Perhaps this was because there was no personal feeling about it. We were like two men in a cell built to hold only one, an uncomfortable situation, but, as neither could go away, one that had to be made the best of.

We also had one casualty in the Divisional Staff, for while Ewart was galloping to a ridge to look for the advanced guard, his horse put his foot in an ant-bear hole, and, coming down, had landed him with his head on a rock, cutting it open rather badly and spraining his right wrist. Luck is a curious thing. When I first met Ewart, in 1885, he was being shot at hard at Kosheh on the Nile; the next time was after Magersfontein, where he was Wauchope's Brigade-Major, and had been under fire at short ranges for about twelve hours without a scratch; and during the interval of fifteen years various enemies had been missing him steadily; yet during the four months we were together in the Ninth Division he was rarely without a bandage on some part of him. Certainly most of these wounds were due to the strange fascination which ant-bear holes seemed to have for his horse, but not all, for, as if to make up for the way in which bullets avoided him, all the most usually harmless things hurled themselves at his body.

Next morning, soon after seven, we came up to the advanced guard, which was bivouacked on the west bank of Hamman's Spruit. About a mile to our left front was the conical Spitz Kop, from which the enemy had retired the night before, and immediately to our front a low rounded ridge, on the further side of which we learnt lay the Kroon Spruit and Tweefontein Farm. About seven miles further ahead (*i.e.*, to the north-east) stretched a jagged range of hills over a 'nek,' in which we could see that our red-clay road passed. To the left of this the rocky Blaauwberg* rose to some 800 or 900 feet, and then, falling to an average height of about 500 feet, ran indefinitely to the north-westward. To the right, after rising from the 'nek' to some 500 feet, the range fell to about 300 feet, and, extending for three miles to the south-east, joined another and less uneven ridge, running at right angles to it for about three miles to the south-west, when it ended in a bold bluff overlooking the Kroon Spruit.

The enemy, which had retired from Spitz Kop,

* This name was incorrectly given in my despatch as Bloemberg.

was almost certain to be holding this position, and information had reached us from several sources that a large force was collected on the further side of it. There was therefore little doubt that a fight was in store for us before we reached Lindley. That place was about twelve miles distant by the direct road over the 'nek'; but we were told that by bearing to the south-east, round the western end of the southern hill, we could strike the Senekal-Lindley road, and reach the latter place in about eighteen miles.

As far as I could see, the country to the right looked easier than that in front of us, and if I had had unlimited time I might have tried it; but we were due at Lindley that day, and although the enemy's position was a very strong one, which would have given two or three divisions enough to do to carry in front, I could, at all events, see the worst of it, and it looked as if it could be turned without marching the whole force for an extra six miles into unknown ground. I therefore settled to accept a fight there.

Leaving the transport (for which Macdonald provided the Highland Light Infantry as escort) in a safe place by Kroon Spruit, we mounted another low ridge out of range of the Boer guns,* but from which Grant estimated that Blaauwberg was within reach of his; so I left him there, pushing on across two more little streams with the infantry and Field

* Most of these guns had a range of 6,000 yards.

Battery towards a slight rise in the ground, from which I thought our field guns would just get their range. I had meant to make a good show in front, and then, extending just out of range, to slip a battalion off to the right down one of the little valleys to occupy the south hill, and thence work round the enemy's left. All this came off as I intended, except the extension out of range. It was not a hazy day, but there must have been something peculiar about the light, for every one of us under-estimated the distance : Grant's knoll proved to be 4,000 yards instead of over 6,000, and, as we soon learnt, the one which I had thought would just bring our field guns in range of the ridge was within that of the enemy's musketry. The Black Watch, which was leading, had marched up to this in line of single rank, and was beginning a wider extension, when little puffs of dust rose at our feet, like that raised by the first heavy drops of a summer storm. I was talking to Macdonald at the time, and, not hearing the familiar whizz of a bullet, did not for a moment realize that we were under fire. It was evidently extreme range fire, and the bullets, falling at an acute angle, were not very deadly ; but there was too much of it to keep the artillery under, unless it was absolutely necessary, so I told Lane to take up another position in rear of the nearest spruit. The Black Watch, having got there, had to stay and hold the front, and had a trying morning ; but owing to their wide extension, and the long

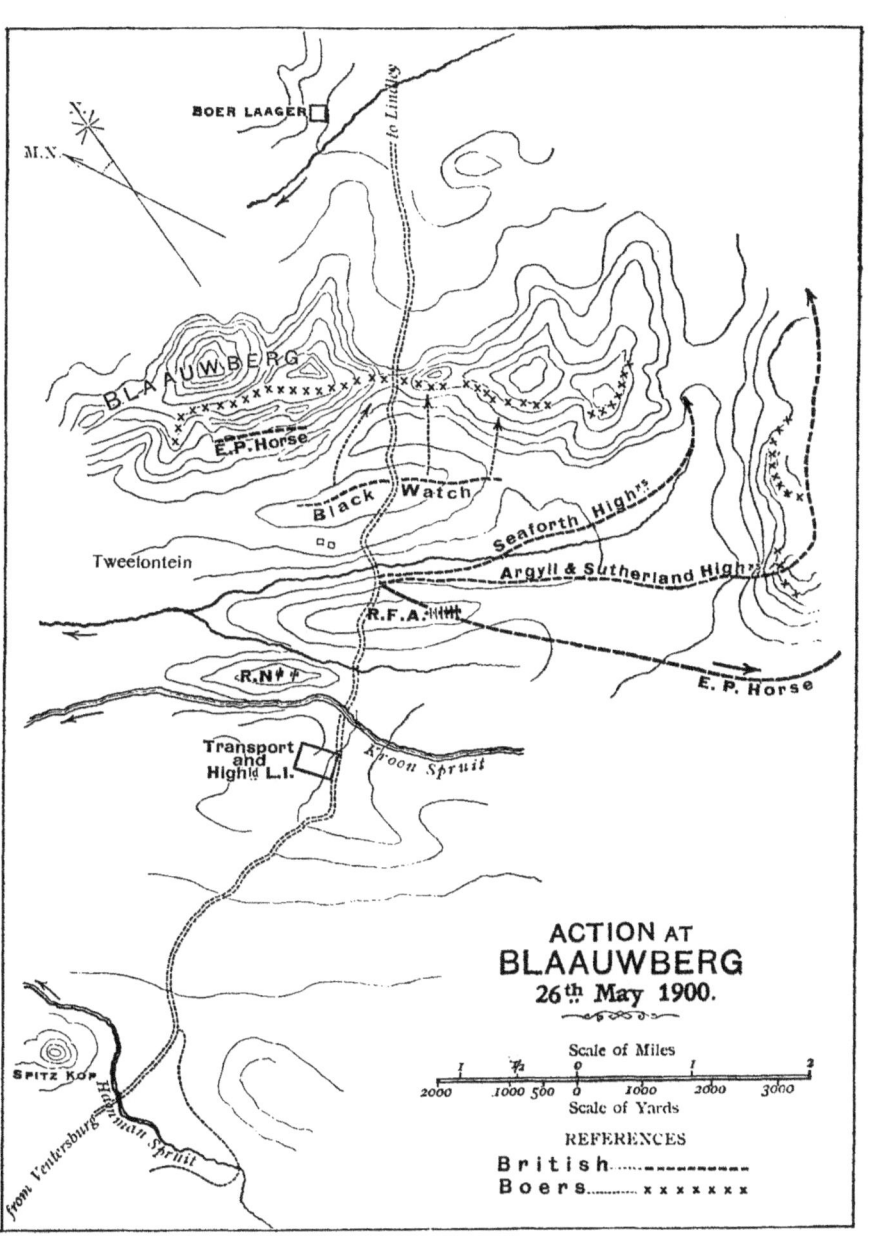

range at which the enemy was firing, till they advanced, they only lost one man killed and nine wounded.

The Eastern Province Horse, whose scouting was very bold, suffered much more heavily in proportion, losing four men killed and eight wounded and six horses, nearly all in the first fusillade.

After this everything went very smoothly. Major Urmston, commanding the Argyll and Sutherland Highlanders, led his battalion along the low ground out of sight of Blaauwberg towards the south hill, which the enemy was found to be holding, but by very clever manœuvring he gained it with the loss of only one man killed and two wounded. This movement was greatly helped by Lieutenant Kirkwood and the remainder of the Eastern Province Horse, who made a wide sweep round the hill. As one commando eventually retired in the Senekal direction, he would have had a good chance of cutting it off had he been stronger; but although thirty-five men may be of great use in moving an enemy as sensitive to its flanks as the Boers were, they cannot be expected to cut off his retreat.

As soon as the Argyll and Sutherlands had gained the south hill, the Seaforths, who had been widely extended to the right rear of the Black Watch, began to move towards the pass at the south-east end of the main range, and all the guns opened fire on the ground to the left of it, keeping down the enemy's fire till they had reached the 'dead ground' at its base. By the time they were in the pass the Argyll and Sutherlands were a couple of thousand yards to their right front, and well round the left of the enemy's main position. The Black Watch then advanced, and the Boers, finding themselves threatened in front, flank and rear, began to retire, only leaving a small rearguard to hold the breastworks on the summit till the last. At half-past eleven the Black Watch had gained the pass and the hills on both sides of it, and the Boers could be seen galloping away to the eastward, while a string of waggons filed out of their laager about two and a half miles to the north.

It was a tantalizing situation, which use had not yet made me contented with. 'If those Yeomanry had only turned up in time——'* we all said, and then built mental pictures, each according to his kind. But the Yeomanry had not turned up, and there was nothing for it but to watch the Boers streaming away, knowing that they need not fight us again till they wanted to.

The action was of course inconclusive—none can be otherwise which lets the enemy go away unmolested; but as far as it went it was satisfactory. We had passed the only barrier on our way to Lindley, and done it with far less loss than I had dared to hope when I first saw what a very strong

* The E.P.H. horses were by this time reduced to eighty; of these, fifty-five were on the flanks.

position it was. No other enemy would have let such a small force as ours do it, and with no other enemy could I have tried to do it in the way I did: for the Boer, with many very strong points, has his limitations, a knowledge of which lets one take liberties with him. He is a good shot (though not so good as we thought before the war), with an inborn talent for choosing a position, a master of the art of taking cover, very mobile, and very clever in the way in which he covers his retreat. But having chosen his position, he rarely leaves it till he is either forced from it or outflanked; he is extraordinarily sensitive as to his flanks, and, in spite of his mobility, rarely changes front to meet an outflanking movement. He never makes a counter-attack, or, having once retired, rallies on the same day.* He can therefore be held in front with a handful of men, which a European enemy would sweep away, and which can afterwards be used to take the position without any fear of their being driven back by a rally. He can always be moved out of a position, if it is small enough to be outflanked in one day; by the second day he will have taken up another to meet a flank march.

We learnt later in the day that the force we had been fighting was made up of the commandos of Commandants Prinsloo and Potgieter, and that the former had retired through Lindley in an easterly

* I am speaking from my own experience; that of others may be different.

direction, while the latter had moved more to the north to effect a junction with Commandant De Wet, whose commando was between Lindley and Heilbron. Commandant Potgieter's commando was also seen moving northwards by the left flanking party of the Eastern Province Horse.

Soon after noon the column formed up and set off again towards Lindley, through a rolling veldt country with higher hills to our right. From these the right flank guard of the Eastern Province Horse saw a body of the enemy with horses, some 200 strong, hidden in a valley to our right rear; as it seemed likely that they were waiting to pounce on our convoy, I sent back the field battery with an escort of half the Argyll and Sutherland Highlanders to a hill about a mile and a half off the road to shell them. Lane dropped a few shells fair into the middle of them, and, as they were closely packed, probably did some damage. At any rate, they retired very hurriedly to the southwards, and the rearguard came in without any adventures.

At half-past three the head of the column reached Lindley, of the occupation of which I had been told in the Military Secretary's telegram of the 18th, and where I had half hoped I might be joined by my Nineteenth Brigade, for I had not been told that the British force had been withdrawn. We soon learnt, however, that it had left six days before (*i.e.*, on the 20th) by the road leading to the north.

The few inhabitants were very anxious to know

whether we had come to stay for good, as they found the alternation of Boer and British rule rather trying, and said that since Hamilton left they had suffered from continual threats and abuse, for helping the English. I was sorry not to be able to satisfy their curiosity, but with De Wet with 3,000 or 4,000 men reported to be ahead of me, Potgieter joining him from my left, and possibly Prinsloo from my right, I thought that the less that was known about our plans, the better.

Although we had telegraph operators with us, as I have said before, we had no instrument; but I hoped to find one in the village, and Gleichen and Colonel Barker rode on with these men, the first to question the inhabitants, and the second to see if it were possible to get into communication with Headquarters; but they found that not only was the wire cut beyond our reach, but that the instrument had been taken away. As we were already rather nearer to Heilbron than to Kroonstad, and hoped to be a good deal nearer next day, I put off sending messages by runner till we were a little further on our road.

Nearly all the Free State villages—or towns, as they are called—are in bad defensive positions for a small force, being built as close to water as possible, and therefore always commanded on at least two sides; but here, besides the valley to which we were accustomed, there was a large isolated hill to the north-east, which commanded the Heilbron road,

I thought, therefore, the sooner we were in a position to occupy it, the better; so leaving a small outpost on the south side of the valley, above the Lindley-Kroonstad road, we crossed the Valsch River, and bivouacked on its north bank. A few shots were fired at the ubiquitous Eastern Province Horse from Kromdrai (a hill to the east), but otherwise we were not disturbed.

The road down to and up from the drift was a very steep one, and it was past sunset before the last of the transport got in and the men could get their dinners. As soon as they had done this, Major Urmston took two companies of the Argyll and Sutherland Highlanders on to the top of the high hill which commanded the Heilbron road. After a hard day's work, I did not like to send the men off for a stiff climb and an uncomfortable night on the rocks without their dinners, but I own I had been in rather a fidget till I knew the hill was in our hands. With a strong force in front of us, the three days which the Chief of the Staff had allowed were not too much for the forty-two or forty-three miles march to Heilbron, and I did not want to spend half one of them in fighting our way out of Lindley, which we should have had to do had the enemy got a gun on to this hill: for they could have raked the transport as it filed out of camp, and made it impossible for us to go on till we had taken it, but with it in our hands there was nothing to stop us. The enemy, it is true, might have occupied some hills to the north-west, but the road was out of range from them, and as we were a flying column, with no communications to keep up, we could have let him stay there; for, as I have said before, a Boer will not leave a good position to come and fight on a bad one.

The following orders were issued for the next day's march :

' LINDLEY,
' 26.5.00.

' 1. The Division will march to-morrow at 7 a.m. moving off from the Highland Brigade bivouac in the following order.

'E.P.H. less six with rearguard.

'Advanced Guard Highland Brig. to be detailed by G.O.C.

'7th Company R.E.

' 1 Battalion Highland Brigade.

'5th Battery R.F.A.

'2 Battalions Highland Brigade.

'Naval Brigade, with one Company H.B. as escort.

' 2nd Line Transport.

'Ox Convoy with 1 Company H.B. as escort.

'7 company H.B. as rear and baggage guard.

'2. The outposts south of the Valsch River will be withdrawn in time to move away with the rearguard and will then join their units.

'3. The S.A.A. will be completed to make up

what was expended to-day and the S.A.A. carts will then fill up from the ox ammunition column.

'4. O.C. units will send in as early as possible casualty lists for the last two days.

'5. Countersign ORANGE.

'6. All animals are to be inspanned and ready to move at short notice, if necessary by daylight to-morrow.'

CHAPTER IX

LINDLEY TO RHENOSTER RIVER

HALF an hour's march on the morning of the 27th took us clear of the hills, and the main body got into the open without any sight of the enemy, though the Military Police, who had been in the town, were fired at as they left it. After crossing some three miles of level, cultivated ground, we came to the edge of a valley, on the further side of which the country began to rise. Here the road divided, and, although the guides were all agreed that the two branches came together later, they differed a good deal as to which was the better one. While they were arguing (with great heat) on this question, it was reported to me that the rearguard was being fired on ; so, as the right-hand road led past a good position on the further side of the valley, I settled to go by that, and wait for the transport to close up. This and crossing the drift* took some time, and, as our march seemed likely to be slow, I told Gleichen that I should send off the messages to the Chief of

* Every valley had a boggy stream which caused a good deal of delay to the transport.

the Staff which I had hoped to telegraph the day before; the first merely reported progress, and the second explained my wants and plans, and this I rewrote to bring it up to date. Although neither of these was delivered, I will quote the second as showing my view of the situation at the time:

'CHIEF OF THE STAFF,
    'ARMY HEADQUARTERS.

'LINDLEY, 27th May, No. 191.—Force under Prinsloo, which I engaged yesterday, reported retired 2 hours Eastward. A strong force under De Wet with thirteen guns is reported to be between me and Heilbron with the intention of disputing my advance. I have insufficient cavalry to scout and protect my long line of transport and if the Yeomanry promised could join me it would be of great assistance. If you have any confirmation of the report as to De Wet a demonstration from Heilbron would probably relieve the pressure on me. My ambulances are full and I have had to clear two ox-wagons for sick. If I have another engagement I shall be seriously hampered in this respect. I expect to be about 15 miles N. of Lindley by this evening. Lieut. Welch 5 M.I. wounded. Lt. Logan N.S.W.M.I. enteric and three men wounded still in Lindley hospital.*
                    'G.O.C. 9TH DIV^N.'

* Left by Hamilton's force.

This was handed to one of the crowd of picturesque ragamuffins we called 'Gleichen's Horse,' and sent off with a covering letter to the 'Officer Commanding' at Heilbron, asking him to telegraph it to the Chief of the Staff. The boy (a Basuto), we afterwards heard, got through to Heilbron, and handed the note to an Englishman whom he found playing lawn-tennis outside the town ; but a Boer policeman had his eye on him, and took possession of it.

After about another five-miles march, we reached the mouth of a steep valley running north and south, and up which the road led to a pass reported by the Eastern Province Horse to be held by the enemy, with whom they were already engaged, one man having had his horse shot under him. They claimed to have emptied several Boer saddles, but were not strong enough to clear the road. The infantry had, therefore, to be extended for attack, and, although they gained the pass and hills on either side of it without serious opposition, this caused some delay.

At a quarter past one we reached De Rust's farm, about three miles beyond the pass, and, receiving a report that Colonel Carthew-Yorstoun, with the rearguard, was heavily pressed by the enemy, I sent back two field guns to his assistance, and parked the First Line Transport by the dam till the convoy and rearguard had closed up. The guns soon cleared the Boers off the rearguard, and at three we moved on again, and had no further dealings with the enemy that day; but the Eastern Province Horse with the rearguard reported that De Rust's farm had been occupied after we left it.

Knowing the delay which even small spruits always caused, I was very anxious to get across the large Rhenoster on that day, so as to make a fair start in the morning; but by the map it was still fully ten miles away, and there did not seem much chance of reaching it. It was, therefore, very good news when, at about half-past four, the guides told us that a little conical 'Spitz Kop,' which was then rising above the sky-line, was on the further side of the river. Half an hour later a line of dark cliffs came in sight, at the foot of which we learnt the Rhenoster ran.

The sun was about to set as we crossed this, and before dark the men had settled down into their bivouac a mile further to the north, outposts were placed on the cliffs overlooking the river, the Eastern Province Horse sent ahead to occupy the 'Spitz Kop,' and everything made snug for the night, and as far as possible for the next day's march. How long this would be it was difficult to judge; the farm by the drift called Groot Krantz* was not marked on the map, the farmer was away 'on commando,' and his wife reticent on all subjects except the high price of eggs. We certainly had not covered the twenty-eight miles shown on the map between Lindley and the Rhenoster, but, as near as

* Great cliff.

we could calculate from our very irregular march, about eighteen, which would leave us twenty-five or twenty-six from Heilbron, or two easy marches for the men. The weather was then cool, and sometimes cold, and they could step out well; but the winter days, which suited them, made havoc with the oxen, who will not graze at night, and were never given time to do so by day. While we were out of touch of the enemy I used to start them off a couple of hours before dawn under a guard, let them have three or four hours' grazing in the middle of the day, and catch us up in the evening; but these last two days' marches from sunrise to sunset had brought about the loss of thirty, among which were some from Grant's picked gun teams. He and Captain Brooks, in charge of the ox convoy, were in despair, and both reported that unless the beasts were given a chance of grazing by daylight they feared they would not get through another march. The sun then rose at twenty minutes to seven, so I settled to give them two hours, and march at half-past eight.

I made the waggon-shed of the farm my Headquarters, and it was still dark inside when next morning a man, whom I at first took to be one of the Eastern Province Horse, handed me a note. Having lit the candle, I read the following:

'COLONEL SPRAGGE TO GEN. COLVILLE.

'Found no one in Lindley but Boers—have 500 men but only one day's food, have stopped three miles back on Kroonstadt road. *I want help to get out without great loss.

'B. SPRAGGE, L^t.-Col.

'27.5.1900.'

My first question after reading this was, 'Who is Colonel Spragge?' of whom I had not before heard, and in answer to this was told that he was the officer commanding the Yeomanry. The next was to make sure of his position, which the message did not seem to make perfectly plain; but this was soon cleared up by the orderly, who explained that the force had entered Lindley, and, finding it occupied, had retired five† miles towards Kroonstad.

I, of course, read the message again several times during the next half-hour, and thought carefully over all it might mean; but the most important part of it, both on first reading and after thinking more carefully over it, seemed to be Colonel Spragge's want of supplies, and my first thought was whether I could help him in that respect. A man does not have long arguments with himself at these moments, but sees his facts arranged on the two sides of the account, so that, although I answered at once, the case presented itself to me somewhat in this form: From the way in which our rearguard had been harassed, the enemy was certainly too strong to let a convoy pass with a small escort, and anything

* Here is an erasure of what appears to be a capital M.
† This was, of course, merely his judgment of the distance.

large enough to be safe would leave us too weak to fight our way to Heilbron; so if a convoy went at all the whole force might as well go with it, and as we had to be at Heilbron next day that could not be thought of. I therefore told the orderly that I could not send the supplies, and asked Murray to see that he and his comrade got some breakfast before taking back my written answer.

I then analyzed the message more carefully, but could find nothing in it to make me change my mind.

The first sentence gave no information. There were only Boers in Lindley when we left it, probably from fifty to a hundred, and the message gave no hint whether there were more or less. As the three commandos that I knew of were said to be on my road, it was not likely that the force would be very large.*

The next sentence seemed to be the most important one—'have 500 men but only one day's food.' Had it read 'have only 500 men and one day's food,' I should have gathered that not only his supplies were limited, but that his force was insufficient to meet that which opposed it. The 'but,' however, conveyed the meaning that his sole anxiety was on the question of supplies. The message 'have a boat but only one oar' would lead the reader to suppose that the sailor lacked nothing

* In his despatch of the 14th August, Lord Roberts says: 'Spragge was at first only opposed by a small force.'

but means of propulsion; 'have only a boat and one oar,' that he needed a bigger craft.

'One day's food' I took to mean one day's rations; that was the sense in which it was generally used. If we wished to state our position more specifically, we wrote 'have' so many days' 'half' or 'one-third rations,' as the case might be. A day's rations at a pinch can be made to last for two, three, or four days.* At Paardeberg the whole army had been for several days on half-rations; we were on half-rations when we reached Winburg; and we were then going on one-third rations, so that to have only one day's rations would not be a serious matter for a mounted force within forty-three miles of Kroonstad, provided that it could move away. Even if the message meant that he had only food to last one day, a small mounted force would have no difficulty in collecting supplies from farms as it went. It will be remembered that I had been told by the Chief of the Staff to supply my 4,000 men in this way in a village which had already supplied 11,000, and with hardly any cavalry to help me. In either case it seemed certain that Colonel Spragge would retire, the more so that neither my own knowledge of the country, nor the results of his conversation with the orderlies—which Gleichen brought me—nor the last sentences of the

* The Yeomanry held out for four days, and the court of enquiry found that they could have held out longer but for an accident independent of supply difficulties.

message, gave any hint that the Yeomanry could not get out at all.

The message said, 'have stopped three miles back on the Kroonstadt road.' I knew that Lindley was a regular trap, and, although I had not actually been over it, I had seen that the country to the west was more open. Having retired from Lindley because of the presence of Boers, it was to be supposed that Colonel Spragge had limited his retirement to three miles, because that was far enough to free him from them for the moment, while the fact that he had been able to send me messages by two men in uniform proved that he could not have been closely invested.

The last sentence of all, however, showed that, if he was not actually in touch with the enemy he expected to be so, but still gave no idea of investment. It did not say that he could not get out, but that he wanted help to do so without great loss. What this loss would probably be was, of course, a matter of conjecture. In European wars regiments have lost 40 to 50 per cent., but, judging by our standard, 10 per cent. was great; and if he had been able to retire from the trap at Lindley without loss, it seemed highly improbable that he would lose anything near that percentage in making his retreat good.

It would be about twenty hours from the time Colonel Spragge had halted before his messengers could return to him, and fully forty before my force could reach him, for we should not only have had to fight our way back to our bivouac on the north of the Valsch River, past the hill which the Argyll and Sutherland Highlanders had held, but over the drift into Lindley, and the further three miles to his camp, so if we reached our old bivouac before dark that day we should have done well. I therefore thought it probable that when his messengers returned to him they would find that he had gone, and almost certain that, whether they reached him or not, he would have retired before we could do so.

However, the fact remained that he had asked for help, and that I was bound to give it to him if I could without sacrificing greater interests. That I could do so by disregarding these, I had no doubt —perhaps with a loss greater than the Yeomanry would have suffered by retiring, certainly at the price of being three days late at Heilbron, and probably of having to retire on Kroonstad for supplies. As long, however, as these things did not clash with the general plan, I should have felt myself free to follow the natural impulse to give help when it is asked for; it was all a question of proportion. It was evident that Colonel Spragge expected to suffer a certain loss in making good his retreat. Whenever a brigade or battalion is sent into action it is with the knowledge that it will suffer loss—maybe great loss—or even that it may be destroyed; but the General who is too soft-hearted to sacrifice a few hundred or thousand men if it is necessary for the general good is as unfitted for his post as the 'butcher' who throws away men's lives merely for the sake of some passing gain that will add to his notoriety.

At that moment one of the most important operations of the war—the passage of the Vaal—was about to take place. I had been told nothing of Lord Roberts's plan, but I had received certain orders,* which gave me what I believed was a clue to them, and the question I had to decide was whether I was justified in throwing the whole machine out of gear, by the absence of one of its parts, in order to save some fifty or even (taking 'great loss' at 20 per cent.) a hundred men. I decided that I was not, and that, at whatever cost, it was my duty to be at Heilbron on the day ordered —the 29th May.

To fulfil this duty and return to Lindley could not be done, and after, as I have shown, turning all sides of the question over in my mind, I only found the more reason to hold to the decision I had formed on first reading the message.

While I was thinking over Colonel Spragge's message, Ewart and Gleichen—whom I had sent for—came, and I told the latter to have a talk with the orderlies, and get all the information he could from them. As soon as he came back and had told me all he had been able to gather, I dictated the following message, which he wrote in Ewart's field note-book (Ewart having sprained his wrist):

* See p. 146.

'28th May.

'COLONEL SPRAGGE, C^g. Imperial Yeomanry.

'Your message received 7 a.m. I am 18 miles from Lindley and 22 from Heilbron, which latter place I hope to reach to-morrow. The enemy are between me and you and I cannot send back supplies. If you cannot join me by road to Heilbron you must retire on Kroonstadt living on country and if necessary abandon your wagons.'

I then signed this, and Gleichen having made two other copies, one was given to each of the orderlies, and the third to a Kaffir named Klas, who knew the country well and wanted to return to his kraal near Lindley. They were ordered to disperse and travel wide apart, but in the afternoon they all came back together, having failed to deliver the message, as they said they could not get through the Boers.

I have tried to give my train of thought at the moment, but had I then known much that I have since learnt, many of my judgments would have been modified, and my actions altogether changed, for I was then ignorant of the two most important factors in the case: (1) that Colonel Spragge believed I had sent for him, (2) that my arrival at Heilbron on the date fixed was unimportant.

1. It was many months afterwards—indeed, not until after I returned to England—that I heard that Colonel Spragge had received a telegram, purporting to come from me, calling on him to follow me to

Lindley.* Even now I do not know the details of this, but there seems to be no doubt that it was received by him at Kroonstad, and that he hurried to Lindley expecting to find me there. That, having sent a messenger after the officer who he believed had called him, he should wait, first for the return of the messenger, and then for the force, which he was hastening to join, is only natural, and fully accounts for his delaying till it was too late to retire. This message, of course, placed him in a very different position to that of an officer commanding a force merely with orders to effect a junction with another.

Although the existence of this telegram fully accounts for Colonel Spragge's action, and makes my forecast faulty, it, of course, in no way affects my reasons for not returning to help him—that is, from a military point of view, which is the only one to be taken in war. Had I known of the telegram at the time it would have made my decision all the harder; but it could not have altered my views of the duty which I owed to Lord Roberts, and the whole army, of which my force and Spragge's were merely items, allotted certain tasks for a common end.

2. That my arrival at Heilbron on the date fixed was unimportant I learnt within the next

* I have also heard that he telegraphed to me at Lindley, but I have no direct evidence on this. If he did, it could only have been while that place was in the hands of the Boers.

few days, when I found that it had been evacuated, that Lord Roberts was across the Vaal, that the main line of the railway was not yet open to the junction, and that Rundle was at Senekal, and therefore still supplied from Winburg. It follows that whether I arrived at Heilbron next day or next day week could have made no difference to the general plan.

What Spragge's orders may have been I never heard, or whether he was told any more about my movements than I was about his; but, as he was presumably in communication with Headquarters till he left the railway, it is still a mystery to me how he can have been allowed to believe that a telegram sent from Lindley, while that place was in Boer hands,* could have come from me, who was known to Headquarters to be still at Ventersburg,† and why, having been ordered to join me at Ventersburg,‡ he was taken thirty miles beyond that place to Kroonstad.

* It is stated that this telegram was dated Lindley, the 23rd May. Hamilton left on the 20th, and I did not arrive till the 26th.

† See Chief of Staff's telegram of 20th May, p. 146.

‡ I understand that part of the Yeomanry derailed at Ventersburg Road Station on the 23rd May and marched to Kroonstad, and that the remainder were detained for some hours at the former place on the 24th owing to a block in the line.

CHAPTER X

ROODEPOORT

THE force moved off at 8.30 on the morning of the 28th, the advanced and rear guards being furnished respectively by the Highland Light Infantry and the Argyll and Sutherland Highlanders. On getting abreast of the Spitz Kop at 9.30, the latter relieved the detachment of Eastern Province Horse, whose comrades had already reported that the enemy was holding Roodepoort, a high ridge over which the road passed some three miles to the front. The Highland Light Infantry was then pushed forward to occupy some kraals and broken ground about 1,200 yards from the enemy's position, which the Field and Naval guns shelled at a range of about 3,000 yards.

I do not know whether the Boers, expecting us to make a turning movement, placed themselves beforehand to meet it, or whether they intended to hem us in; but, at any rate, they did not hold Roodepoort with any stubbornness, but, as will be seen later, threw all their strength on to our flanks and rear, so that by eleven the Highland Light

Infantry, under cover of fire from the batteries, gained the crest with a loss of only two men. They were to have been supported by the Black Watch, but after the latter had followed them for about a thousand yards it was seen that the enemy was threatening our left, and they were detached to meet the attack, their right resting on a kopje at the west end of the Roodepoort ridge, and their left on some rolling ground to the south-westward. This left a gap of some 1,500 yards between their right and the left of the Highland Light Infantry, which I had to close as far as possible with Kincaid's half-company of Royal Engineers.

At the same time that the Highland Light Infantry and Black Watch were sent to threaten Roodepoort, the Seaforths were moved off to make a wide turning movement to the right, their line of advance running along the north-western side of a valley hidden from the Roodepoort ridge. Soon after eleven they were heavily attacked from the right rear by a force which far outnumbered them, but, advancing on to some higher ground, held their own all day, although they were not strong enough to make any counter-attack.

With the attack on the Seaforths came another most determined one from the right and rear on the Argyll and Sutherlands, whose right* rested on Spitz Kop and their left on a kraal in the plain. This was held by the Volunteer company, which

* *I.e.*, proper right facing northwards.

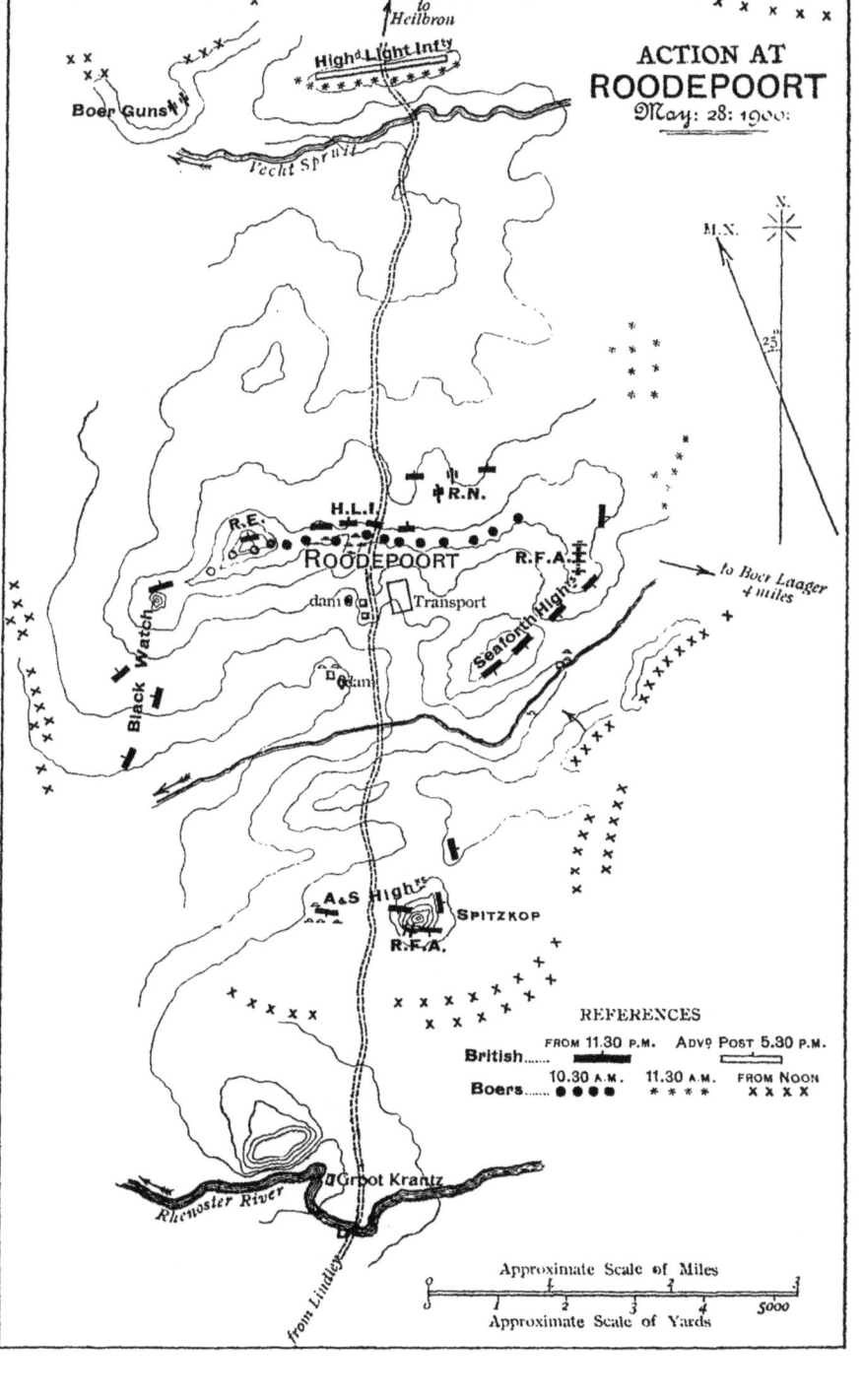

drove back a series of attacks and warded off several attempts to turn their flank. They had the good luck to see the Boers at their boldest, and made the best use of their chance.

As soon as the enemy left Roodepoort, I ordered the two batteries to advance, except two guns, which were then detached to support the Argyll and Sutherland on Spitz Kop. Even with the help of these the rearguard was unable to drive back the enemy, which pressed it closely till night fell.

On reaching the top of Roodepoort, we could see that the enemy from that part of the field had retired to the north and north-east, those in the former direction being on the further side of the Vecht Spruit.* As they offered a good target, I brought up the Field Battery; but it had hardly time to get into position before shells began to fly past us from two guns which we could then make out rather to the west of the men and horses we had seen. As Lane found out that they were beyond his range, I ordered him to withdraw, and, on hearing a little later how things were going with the Seaforths, sent the battery to support them, and with its help the enemy was driven off our right by about a quarter past three.

If, for a wonder, Grant was not in front, he was never far behind, and in spite of a very steep pull up to this ridge he did not keep us waiting for

* An affluent of the Rhenoster River, for which it is evidently mistaken in the Intelligence Department map.

many minutes. His Four Point Sevens soon made themselves felt, and after about half a dozen rounds the Boer guns limbered up and vanished behind a spur. The Naval guns remained in this position all day, dropping a shell into the enemy whenever he gave a good target, generally at ranges of from 5,000 to 6,000 yards. We met a Field-Cornet at Heilbron who had been wounded by one of these shells, some of which he said had been remarkably effective. This was the only time during the war that I had any direct evidence as to the results of our artillery fire.

As soon as our right was clear, Macdonald advanced the Highland Light Infantry on to a spur about half-way between Roodepoort and the Vecht Spruit, and I ordered the Eastern Province Horse to push over the spruit, and reconnoitre the ground to the north, from which, as far as we could make out, the enemy had retired into the hills to the north-east. If this proved to be the case, I proposed to push on a battalion to hold this ground, and secure our passage of the drift next morning; but we did not know whether there was water near any good position. It was then four o'clock, and the next ridge was a good four miles away, so the Eastern Province Horse could hardly send a messenger back in time to let me start off the battalion to reach its position before dark. They had no signallers, and if I had only had my divisional unmounted ones to work with, I could not have learnt all I wanted in time, and should have either had to risk letting the battalion bivouac in the valley or losing the command of the drift. Luckily, Macdonald, by some means which he did not confide to me, had got hold of ponies on which to mount two of his brigade signallers,* and, these having been handed over to Kirkwood, the party cantered off.

The sun then set at a quarter past five, and there were clouds on the horizon, and even with the mounted signallers it was a chance if we got the message through. With our glasses we watched the party canter down the slope, disappear into the drift, and then more slowly (much too slowly, we thought) mount the opposite slope; then they were hidden behind some fold in the ground, and the sun sank behind a bank of cloud. I expressed my feelings in one syllable, and was turning away in disgust, when I heard Browne say, 'We've got them.' The sun had forced its way for a moment through a rift in the cloud-bank, and Kirkwood just had time to signal 'Good water in dam' before it disappeared for the night.

The Highland Light Infantry, who had been warned, were packed off at once, and we could just make them out near the top of the further slope before it got dark. As soon as we knew that they had secured the drift, the ox transport was sent forward to outspan on the north side of it. This not only gave them a little more time for grazing in

* Macdonald told me afterwards that having these mounted signallers always at hand alone enabled him to direct satisfactorily the movements of his very extended brigade during this march.

the morning, but saved the delay they would have caused had we had to wait while they crossed it; for, after the last two days' experience, I could hardly expect that the rearguard would be left alone.

The Argyll and Sutherland were still engaged, but only an occasional shot from the battery showed that there were any Boers left on our right front, while the force opposed to the Black Watch had long ceased to trouble them; it seemed to have withdrawn to reinforce that attacking the rearguard. The left, therefore, only wanted the usual outposts, and the Black Watch was withdrawn and formed up under the southern crest of Roodepoort, near a dam where I had parked the mule transport and guns. I could not move these on to the northern slope, which was exposed to artillery fire from the further side of the Vecht Spruit, until Rustfontein (the farm which the Highland Light Infantry had occupied) was in our hands, and it was then too late to do it by daylight. On the other hand, I could not give up Spitz Kop until the transport were safely over Roodepoort, so the Argyll and Sutherland had to stay where they were. In any case it is doubtful whether they could have withdrawn by daylight without more loss than it would have been worth. The Seaforth, though not pressed, were still in touch with the enemy, and they were also in a good position from which to take their place on the next day's march; so they also bivouacked on the ground they had held all day.

The result of this was a very extended bivouac, of which the front and rear faces were formed by the Highland Light Infantry and the Argyll and Sutherland, seven miles apart, and the sides by the Seaforth and the Black Watch outposts, three miles apart.

The day had been a trying one, and with less trustworthy troops might have ended badly for us; but the Highlanders, who had always been ready to go ahead against any odds, had by this time picked up a good many wrinkles from their enemies, and were as clever as the Boers in making the best use of ground. The excellent practice of the two batteries had enabled us to clear Roodepoort with hardly any loss, and later the Naval guns had kept those of the enemy at a distance, while the Field Battery had removed the pressure on the Seaforth, and materially helped the Argyll and Sutherland to hold their own. The Eastern Province Horse, by this time reduced to thirty-five mounted men, had enabled us to seize the advanced position. The result was not very great in mileage, for although the advanced guard had covered nearly ten miles, the rearguard was barely three from its bivouac of the night before. It was some comfort, however, to know that we had gained some ground, and a great one to learn, as I did shortly, that our total casualties were only thirty-three. Among these was Colonel Hughes-Hallett, who was, however, only slightly wounded.

From information which Gleichen afterwards collected at Heilbron, he reported that the force against us was over 5,000 strong, and was composed of the commandos of Commandants Steinkamp, Netley, P. De Wet, C. De Wet and Oliver, and was accompanied by President Steyn. Although I did not know these details at the time, it was clear that, if the enemy was as pressing on the morrow as he had been all day, we should have our work cut out to reach Heilbron up to time. The Boers had been so bold in some of their advances, especially against the rearguard, that I believed that they must have suffered more than usual; but there were certainly enough of them to delay us a good deal.

I do not think either Macdonald or I owned, even to ourselves, the possibility of failing to get through in the next day; but we had some sixteen or eighteen miles to do,* which was not a bad march even without fighting, and I thought that I ought to let Headquarters know how we stood, so that, if by any chance we did not keep our time, they would be prepared to act. I therefore dictated the following message:

'CHIEF OF THE STAFF,
    'ARMY HEADQUARTERS.

'Roodepoort 18 miles S. of Heilbron, 28 May, 5 p.m. No. 194. Have fought on last four days

---

* My Headquarters and the transport were four miles north of the Rhenoster.

and to-day have only marched four miles owing to enemy contesting every position to my front and seriously harassing my rear and right flank. He has 2 guns which out-range my field Battery. I have only 35 mounted men left, two days' food and about 150 rounds per man S.A.A. Enemy are still in force round me and I fear my progress will be very slow. Had report from Colonel Spragge Imperial Yeomanry this morning that he entered Lindley yesterday coming under heavy fire and retired about 5 miles. As owing to enemy between us he could not join me here I sent him orders to do so at Heilbron, if possible by a westerly route or failing that to retire on Kroonstadt. If I fail to reach Heilbron by to-morrow morning it will be because I am stopped by superior force and shall require assistance. Have had about sixty casualties in these four days and ambulances have long been full. Colonel Hughes-Hallett and Lieutenants Doig and Radcliffe Seaforths slightly wounded, Lieutenant Bertram E.P.H. prisoner.

'G.O.C. 9TH DIVISION.'

This message, as I have said, was intended to forewarn the Chief of the Staff, in case we did not reach Heilbron in time, and did not say that I required assistance, but that if I failed to reach Heilbron by the next day I should require it; as I learnt afterwards, on its receipt Methuen was despatched to my rescue. Possibly this view was formed in consequence of the severe opposition Hamilton's force had met with at the same place a week before.*

As we had been less pressed on our left flank than on any other side, I thought the best chance of getting this through was to send it to the railway, and told Gleichen to give it to one of his men; but the natives all said that we were too closely surrounded, and were afraid to go alone. Sergeant Bettington, however, of the Cape Mounted Rifles, who was attached to the Intelligence Department, volunteered to take it, and started off with a Kaffir who pretended to know the road. We learnt afterwards that, having passed safely through the Boer lines, he bolted with his escort's horse and rifle, and left Sergeant Bettington to make his way for twenty-eight miles on foot as best he might.

For the sake of those readers who do not know Sergeant Bettington, I may say that the message was safely delivered; those who do know him will never have had any doubt about it. He had first turned up at Modder River Camp —how or why I do not know—and varied the monotony of those dull days by his habit of appearing unexpectedly outside our outpost line after a stroll through the Boer lines. After a time our sentries got accustomed to him, and did not shoot at him any more. When the reports that 'a man in the uniform of the Cape Mounted Rifles

* See Lord Roberts' despatch of the 14th August, 1900.

was discovered,' etc., ceased to come in, I am ashamed to say that I forgot all about him till, on the morning we attacked Cronje's laager at Paardeberg, a figure which I recognised ran past me at early dawn. It happened that we were then in doubt as to whether a certain trench on the riverbank was held by the Boers or not, and on seeing him, I at once said, 'Why, here is the very man to find out,' and, calling him back, asked if he would do so. 'All right, sir,' said Bettington, with the cheerful smile which any chance of extra danger always brought on to his face, and started off at the 'double.' My Intelligence officer was with me at the time, and said nothing, but the next time I saw Sergeant Bettington he was in charge of 'Gleichen's Horse.'

At dusk the two orderlies and the Kaffir came in, having, as I have said, failed to get through. They were attached to the Eastern Province Horse, and stayed with us at Heilbron till Methuen came there.

CHAPTER XI

THE LAST MARCH

AT 5.45 on the morning of the 29th the transport and Black Watch left the Headquarter bivouac and moved towards the Vecht Spruit Drift, while the Seaforths at the same time left their bivouac; but the Highland Light Infantry stood fast until the column had closed up, and the Argyll and Sutherlands held Spitz Kop till the last of the waggons was over Roodepoort.

The enemy's main laager had been made out just before sunset four miles to the east of the Seaforths' position; and the southern end of a long range of hills on the east of the Heilbron road, and running parallel to it at a distance of about 6,000 yards, was reported by the Eastern Province Horse to be strongly held. There were no signs of the enemy on our left flank, and we had no information as to what was in front of us; but Vecht Kop, a high bluff about seven miles to our left front, was evidently a strong position. This might have to be dealt with later, but for the moment the two most important things to think of were getting the transport safely over the Vecht Spruit and guarding our right and right rear. The Seaforths were doing the latter, and, to secure the former, I told Macdonald that I wished the rearguard to hold Roodepoort till the transport was well on to the high ground to the north of the Vecht Spruit. The Field Battery moved with the Black Watch, but in order to avoid having both the Naval guns in the valley at the same time, I asked Grant to send one on with the transport, and to keep the other on Roodepoort till he saw that the first was across the drift. I stayed with him for some time to see how the rearguard fared. As it was soon evident that the enemy was leaving it alone, it seemed probable that he had given up his plan of trying to surround us, and meant to concentrate all his force in front of us.

The transport was nearly all across the drift by the time I reached it, and about 1,500 yards beyond it I found the Highland Light Infantry extended across the road, and the Black Watch ready to move off as a right-flank guard, the Seaforths being further to the right rear.

We were on a fairly flat upland, whose northern edge, some six miles off, was bounded by a smooth-topped ridge, short of which there did not seem to be any good positions. To our right ran the range I have already mentioned, from the lower slopes of which small bodies of the enemy came shyly forward, keeping out of our rifle range; some eight or nine miles to the north-east its outline was cut by another member of the prolific Spitz Kop family.

I found Macdonald at Rustfontein Farm busy cross-examining the farmer's wife. A talk with him confirmed my views; from all that he had heard and seen, it was clear that the enemy held the range to our right in force, and that we should not meet with much opposition in front, for some hours, at all events. If I had been ordered to clear the country between Lindley and Heilbron, I should have attacked the position on our right, but as it was, I merely had orders to be at Heilbron that day, which was already several hours old; I therefore settled that if the Boers would leave me alone I would do the same for them, and as soon as the rearguard had closed up ordered an advance northwards. With the enemy in force on our right, and possible attacks in front and rear to look out for, the whole Highland Brigade was employed as advanced, rear, and right-flank guard to our three miles of transport. This arrangement was safe enough at first; but at about half-past nine the enemy was seen on Vecht Kop, and as Macdonald had no troops to spare for the left, Kincaid and his Engineers had to look after that quarter, but were reinforced later by half a battalion of the Seaforths.

At ten o'clock the Eastern Province Horse reported the enemy on the ridge ahead of us, and while the Highland Light Infantry advanced towards it, I brought up the Artillery to a knoll from which they could shell it. The Highlanders, however, met with no opposition, and gained it as the guns came into position, and at the same moment came under a heavy enfilade fire from those of the enemy on Spitz Kop, about 7,000 yards to the right of the road. This must have been quite a surprise for the Highlanders, but they certainly did not show it; even at the first shell not a man changed his steady pace to the front, and while shot after shot swept along their ranks, or struck the ground a few yards ahead of them, there was never the faintest sign of hesitation, and the line pressed steadily forward, without a check, till the crest was gained.

The Boer·guns were of course far out of range of the field batteries, but Grant, who was ready to shell the ridge, was not many seconds in laying his guns on to the new target. The first two rounds were high, but the brown cloud that rose from Spitz Kop after his third was almost exactly in the place where the sailor's telescope showed the gun to be, and the Boers' fire soon became wild, and then ceased.

This was satisfactory as far as it went, but it was not likely that the Boer guns were all disabled, and the road passed over the ridge within easy range of Spitz Kop. Boers have a way of lying low till they get their chance, and I felt certain that as soon as the Naval guns moved the enemy's would open fire again, when they could take them at a disadvantage, and also pound the transport as it passed over the ridge.

In nine cases out of ten South African roads follow the natural and only practicable line, but this one looked as if it was an exception to the rule, for the ridge began to fall away about 1,000 yards to the west of the road, which seemed to climb over it, for no better reason than that of going straight. I therefore sent a Staff Officer to see if the inevitable spruit, which ran at the foot of the ridge, was passable, and, on hearing that it was, ordered guns and transport to bear away to the left and keep out of range.

A more enterprising enemy would have met this very simple move by advancing his guns, but the Boers did not, and the transport never came within range. The party on Vecht Kop had retired before the Seaforths, and although a few horsemen were seen hanging about our left flank, they never came within rifle range. Parties of the enemy also followed the rearguard, but seemed shy.

From the ridge on which the Highland Light Infantry had been shelled we could see below us a broad valley falling to the westward out of the Spitz Kop range. At its bottom, some two miles off, was a farm and dam, which proved to be one of the many Rietfonteins, and some three miles beyond it, to the northward, another ridge, over which the road passed between two black kopjes.

As soon as they reached a good position I again separated the Naval guns, telling Grant to leave one with the rearguard until the leading one was out of the hollow. This was not till about half-past two, by which time Macdonald had extended the whole of his brigade, except the rearguard, to cover about four miles of front, the flanks being slightly thrown back, the Highland Light Infantry in the centre, and the Black Watch on the right and the Seaforths on the left.

In this formation they swept up the northern slope of the valley, the Highland Light Infantry gaining the crest without opposition at half-past three, when, seeing that a body of the enemy was advancing from Spitz Kop, evidently to harass the transport, two companies of the Black Watch were detached to meet it. They never came within rifle range of the Boers, but the enemy's guns opened fire on the Black Watch from Spitz Kop at a range of about 6,000 yards, dropping their shells well among them, but doing no harm.

While this demonstration was being made from Spitz Kop, there were signs of a more determined attack from our immediate right, on which a considerable force of the enemy could be seen about 3,000 yards off, advancing along the crest of the ridge. Macdonald at once occupied the two kopjes on either side of the pass; the right one with half a battalion of the Highland Light Infantry, and the left with half the Seaforth. Grant's leading gun was then toiling up the hill, and could not be with us for some time, and the Field Battery, which was in rear of the Seaforth, was about half a mile back to the west of the road; but, on getting a message from me, Lane advanced at a gallop, and was soon in action on the western kopje, making such good practice that the Boers, who we saw had also got a field gun with them, soon retired. Another body then appeared slightly to the right of our front, and while Lane was dealing with these a third body to our left front.

When we gained the pass without opposition, I had thought that we were sure to do the four remaining miles before dark, but this looked as if the last few miles would be the most troublesome ones. It also made me wonder what the English garrison we expected to find at Heilbron was doing.

The sound of the field guns soon brought up Grant, the oxen of whose leading gun were putting their best feet forward only a few hundred yards back, and, seeing a knoll to our left front which was rather less steep than the kopje, I told him to take up a position on that; but it turned out not to be a good one, as a fold in the ground hid the Boers to the left from him, and, as Lane had already dispersed those on the right, he did not get a shot. During the march, or, rather, the last four days of it, his two guns had fired eighty-two rounds, and the field battery 258. Not knowing what might be in store for us, after the 26th we had been very careful of ammunition, and had fired very few rounds at mere positions.

We waited on this ridge for the transport to close

up, and at a quarter to four the force advanced. Two more ridges had to be crossed, but we met with no further opposition. The distance was short, but both men and animals were tired, and the way seemed very long.

Just after sunset I wanted to speak to Macdonald about something, but was told by the advanced guard that he was on ahead, so pushed on, and finally overtook him with his Aide-de-Camp and Brigade-Major cantering towards the town. At that moment a buggy, with two men in it, was seen a hundred yards ahead coming towards us, and one of the Staff, galloping forward, came back with the news that the buggy held the Landdrost of Heilbron, and a minute afterwards Mr. Rous came up on foot. He gave us the startling news that the British troops had left a week ago, and that a small Boer commando was then moving out of the town. He was driving out, he said, to visit his farm, and this naturally led him to the subject of compensation, which he said Hamilton had promised him for some damage to his wire fencing. I, however, had to turn him on to the more immediately pressing question of water-supply and camping-grounds, and having got some general ideas from him on the subject, Barker and Cuthbertson pushed on—the first to make arrangements for the former, and the second for the latter—while Gleichen and Raymond cantered on to take possession of the town. They reported that the inhabitants did not seem particularly pleased to see them, finding, as those at Lindley had done, that the only effect of a short visit from us was to make the Boers suspect them. Not knowing how long we were going to stay, they were very reticent, and Gleichen could get little information. Having seen to the water-supply, Barker had also gone into the town, where he had found the telegraph-office with an instrument in it. The wires were cut, but it was arranged to send out a party to try to mend them the first thing in the morning, for the state of our rations made us anxious to get into communication with Headquarters as soon as possible.

It was seven o'clock, and therefore pitch dark, before the head of the column halted, and half-past eight when the rearguard closed up. Everybody was tired, for the whole day's march had been in extended order over rough ground, and some of the troops on the flanks had made wide détours; but we had just managed to keep our time, and the men, who did not guess, as I already did, that it was all for nothing, were in the best of spirits; all they knew was that Lord Roberts had ordered them to be there on the twenty-ninth, and they would rather have walked their feet off than let it be said that the Highland Brigade could not do anything that it was ordered.

Writing on the conduct of his brigade throughout the march from Ventersburg, Macdonald said: 'I cannot speak too highly of the behaviour of the

THE LAST MARCH

Brigade; their coolness and discipline throughout this long and trying march was most marked, and only for their cheerful determination to overcome all obstacles, and gain their destination on the date appointed by Lord Roberts, I feel certain the distance could not have been completed in the face of the opposition met with.'

I have only one remark to add to this—in which I am sure I shall be borne out by the officers and men of the brigade—that even their 'cheerful determination to overcome all obstacles' would have availed them little but for the energy and resourcefulness of their Brigadier.'

CHAPTER XII

HEILBRON

OUR bivouac-ground had been chosen overnight chiefly for its nearness to the water-supply, but it was commanded on all sides at a range of only a few hundred yards, and the first thing to be done next morning was to choose, and move into, a better defensive position. This was found near the railway-station, to the west of the town. Although better, it was far from good, being also commanded by hills within artillery range. There was a good position, however, for the Naval guns, and we knew they could generally keep those of the Boers quiet, so that, as far as the enemy were concerned, I felt quite at ease. A far more serious question was that of supplies. We had only been rationed, as I have said, to Heilbron, and had therefore naturally expected to find troops and supplies there; instead of which we only found five officers and 216 men of Hamilton's sick and wounded being fed by the townspeople.

The Supply officers at once went round the town and collected what they could, which was enough for

HEILBRON

our immediate wants. But the first round was not very satisfactory; the people were still shy of showing themselves too friendly, for of course there were many among them who would report all that they did to the Boer leaders. They had also their own wants to think of, and, knowing the general situation pretty well, probably looked upon a siege as by no means unlikely. Later I had to order a house-to-house search, and got enough to keep us going, though, except just after Methuen had escorted a convoy in, we could rarely issue more than half, and sometimes only one-third, rations. At noon Barker reported that the wire was mended, that he was in telegraphic communication with Kroonstad, and that the telegrams which I had given him were being sent. The first of these were to the Director of Supplies and the Chief of the Staff explaining our position, and asking that a convoy might be sent as soon as possible. Later in the day I had the following answer from the latter:

'GERMISTON.

'Clear line.

'From C. of S.   To G.O.C., 9th Division, Heilbron.'

'May 30th, 444.—Your 104[*] convoy of rations forage ammunition both small arms and field gun is ready for you at Railhead, please communicate with Railhead regarding its despatch to you. The

* A mistake for 204.

only escort available at Railhead is Lovat's Scouts unless your Yeomanry have got there you should therefore arrange to meet the convoy and give it sufficient escort in your neighbourhood.'

Germiston was not marked on any map which we had, but I found out from one of the inhabitants that it was a suburb of Johannesburg, and it was therefore evident that Lord Roberts had crossed the Vaal. The position of Rail-head, towards which I was told to send an escort for the convoy, was more doubtful, so I telegraphed to the Railway Staff Officer at Kroonstad for information on this point, and learnt in due course that it was at Roodevaal, about thirty miles to the west of Heilbron, and thirty-two south of Wolvehoek junction.

In answer to the Chief of the Staff's telegram, I said that I had no cavalry at Heilbron to escort the convoy, and suggested that it should be escorted by my Yeomanry if they had returned to the railway, or otherwise by Methuen's mounted troops, and that I considered the escort should have long-range guns with it.

In the afternoon the leading inhabitants called on me, and Mr. Rous having resigned the appointment of Landdrost given him by Hamilton, I asked if any of the others would care to take it; but, although they were all Englishmen, they said that, having taken the oath of allegiance to President Steyn, they could not accept any appointment under the British

Government till he absolved them from it. I therefore telegraphed to the Military Secretary, telling him that there were no local applicants for the post, and asking for instructions, as by his telegram about the Winburg Landdrost I was forbidden to appoint one. Some days afterwards the Military Governor of Bloemfontein telegraphed to ask the date on which Lieutenant Huddlestone took up his appointment as Assistant-Commissioner. This may possibly have had some connection with the subject, but, as Lieutenant Huddlestone did not arrive at Heilbron while I was there, I do not know definitely.

I also asked these leading citizens to help us in collecting supplies, which they promised to do, but it was perhaps natural that they should not be very enthusiastic about it.

Later in the day I had two telegrams from Methuen, the first saying that he had been sent to help me, and asking whether I had any need of help or provisions, and whether he could help in any way as regards my Yeomanry; and the second that he had received instructions to relieve the Yeomanry at Lindley after relieving my force, but, as he assumed I was safe, he was proceeding in the direction of Lindley with his Yeomanry brigade and battery. He asked what force Spragge had under him, and if I knew the strength of the enemy round him.

In reply, I told him that I had no need of infantry reinforcements, and that I believed my Yeomanry had retired from Lindley, Spragge having 500 men with him. I also told him of my suggestion to the Chief of the Staff, that his mounted troops with guns should escort my convoy.

In the meanwhile I had heard from the Commandant at Rail-head that he had no mounted troops, and only sixty men of the Highland Brigade available for an escort ; but next day he telegraphed that another hundred Highlanders had arrived, and that, as he considered an escort of 160 sufficient, he should start the convoy of sixty waggons on the following morning.

To this I answered :

' I consider your proposal of escorting with 160 men wholly inadequate. By latest reports I am in presence of 7,000 of enemy and do not feel justified in detaching a large portion of my force on convoy duty. My whole force had its hands full to get here. Please refer question of escort to Chief of the Staff. I have asked Methuen to help but do not know whether he will be available.'

This crossed a message from the Commandant at Rail-head, dated the 1st June, saying that he had delayed the departure of the convoy, as he had heard that I wanted 550 boxes of small-arm ammunition and 990 rounds of 15-pounder ammunition, and was waiting till they were ready. On receipt of this I wrote a telegram asking him to acknowledge the receipt of my previous telegram, as I was anxious to make certain that the convoy had not started without adequate escort, but before we could get it off the wire was cut. I therefore sent the following message in by runner to Rail-head, and had an acknowledgment of its receipt from the Commandant, dated the 3rd June :

'Clear the line.
'Chief of the Staff.
'Military Secretary.
'Army Headquarters.

'N. 230. June 2, Heilbron.—With reference to my 199 and your 32 the enemy has now two guns in position to the E. and S.E. range about 6,000 yards and I expect more. He evidently intends to contain us here. In view of the serious moral effect which would result from the capture of the convoy I consider every precaution should be taken to prevent such an occurrence and that it should be escorted by a force equal to a Brigade of Infantry with mounted troops and guns. D.M.I. wires in his R. 131 "only 3,500 of enemy in your neighbourhood." This does not agree with local information. I advise main road from Prospect for convoy. Please let me know earliest date on which I can expect convoy, that I may calculate allowance of food. Men are on half rations.
'GEN. COLVILE.'

Although I hoped that all my telegrams would have had the effect of stopping the convoy till it could get a proper escort, I told Gleichen to have his men on the look-out for it, and this was done on the 2nd, 3rd, and 4th, the boys, who answered to the names of Robbie, Joseph, April, and Klein Bouy lying out some seven or eight miles, with orders to hasten in and warn us if the convoy was sighted; but nothing was heard till the 5th, when one of them reported that it had been captured on the previous day.

On the 13th June Civil Surgeon Connacher, who had been taken prisoner with the convoy, was returned to us by President Steyn, and told us its story. He said that the convoy, with an escort of 160 infantry, had left the railway near Roodevaal on the evening of the 2nd June, and had trekked (with one long halt) till eight on the following morning; then, after halting till one in the afternoon, had marched till five, when it had outspanned to the north of the Elands Spruit, near Zwaal Krantz (*i.e.*, nine miles from the railway and fourteen from Heilbron on the Prospect-Heilbron road). There, seeing that there were Boers to the right and front, the commanding officer had sent runners to Heilbron and Vredefort for help,* and had extended the men and dug rifle-pits.

They were not molested during the night, but at seven o'clock on the morning of the 4th the Boers sent in a message under a white flag calling on the

* None reached Heilbron. Vredefort was a station on the railway nine miles distant.

officer commanding the party to surrender. As the enemy was 4,000 strong, with several guns, he agreed to do this, only stipulating that the mails which he was bringing for the division should be forwarded to Heilbron. This condition was not fulfilled, as the mails were all burnt. Surgeon Connacher said that before leaving Roodevaal the Commandant and the officer commanding the convoy had discussed my telegram to the effect that I considered that the proposed escort was inadequate.

I had been almost afraid at the time that I was repeating my assertion that it was unsafe to send the convoy with so small an escort to the point of wearisomeness, but having before me the Chief of the Staff's 'Circular Memorandum,' No. 17, which laid great stress on this subject, I saw that it was one to which Lord Roberts evidently attached great importance. Paragraph 5 of this memorandum said: 'Whenever it is known or suspected that bodies of the enemy are in the neighbourhood, all movement of convoys is to be suspended, unless a sufficient escort can be provided. . . . In South Africa, where the enemy possess the most intimate knowledge of every feature of the country, and is prompt to take advantage of isolating and overwhelming small detachments, the neglect of these elementary military precautions is certain to lead to most unfortunate complications, as has been exemplified on several recent occasions.'

As the Chief of the Staff had telegraphed that

the Lovat's Scouts were at Rail-head, I had been rather surprised to hear from the Commandant there that he had no mounted troops. That mystery was, however, partly cleared by the arrival of that corps on the 2nd June. We had heard from natives the day before of a mounted force to the south, and taking it for granted that this must be the Yeomanry, I had sent a message by runner addressed to Colonel Spragge telling him to strike the railway, and act as escort to the convoy. The boy returned next day saying he could not find any troops, and in the meantime the Scouts had marched in. It appeared that, having failed to get any news of the Ninth Division at Ventersburg, they had marched northwards till they fell in with Methuen's column near Kroonstad, and, hearing that he was going to our relief, had joined him till he turned southwards to help the Yeomanry at Lindley. They then left him and marched into Heilbron.

We were very glad to see the Lovat's Scouts, and this addition to my mounted troops was very welcome; but, having brought no supplies with them, they were so many more mouths to feed, and when we heard of the loss of the convoy the supply difficulty looked as if it might be a serious one. I ordered a house-to-house search for food, and having scraped together everything they could find, the Supply officers reported that we had two and a third days' rations of flour and groceries—*i.e.*, seven days on one-third rations—for the men; but we were very short of forage, and, as the force was not large enough to provide an extended outpost line, the grazing-ground was very limited, and was rapidly getting eaten up. The Boers probably realized that this would be one of our difficulties, for they burnt all the grass up to our outposts, so that even if we had got more troops they would have been no help in that respect.

As soon as I heard of the loss of the convoy I asked the Chief of the Staff to send another, but I did not know whether he would be able to do so; and it seemed that the time had come to have it settled definitely what we were expected to do when our rations ran out. I therefore telegraphed to the Chief of the Staff, telling him that on one-third ration of flour and groceries we could hold out till the 14th, or, by eating mules and trek oxen, for three weeks longer, but that many of the mules would soon die, and all be unfit for work, and asked whether Lord Roberts wished us to hold out to the end, or fight our way to the railway. I suggested that, if we were to take the latter course, it would be better to do so while the transport could still move.

This telegram answered itself, for the time, by the arrival next day of Methuen's column. He left again on the following day, taking with him the Black Watch and two guns as an escort for the convoy, which he promised to send from the railway. In the meanwhile he gave us two days' full rations to go on with.

On the day after he left I had a telegram from the Chief of the Staff, saying that Methuen was marching from Lindley to Heilbron, and that it was most important that I should communicate with him with the least possible delay, as De Wet was holding the railway five miles west of Rhenoster Bridge, and that Lord Roberts depended on him to clear the enemy out of his present position on the railway.

While this column was with us, General Douglas, commanding the Ninth Brigade, which formed part of it, told me that on the 24th May he had received a telegram addressed to the 'G.O.C. Ninth Brigade,' telling him to march without the Yeomanry. As he had seen that the address was evidently a mistake for 'G.O.C. Ninth Division,' he had redirected it to me at Ventersburg. I had left Ventersburg before daylight on the 24th, and therefore had not received it; but it came to hand a week after this conversation (June 20th) among a bundle of undelivered telegrams, and ran as follows:

'May 24th.—Yeomanry are so late they cannot catch you at Ventersburg. You must march without them; they will join you later viâ Kroonstadt.—C. of S.'

Had I received this in time, it would not have led me to expect the Yeomanry at Lindley, for, as they were coming from Bloemfontein, they must have passed Ventersburg to get to Kroonstad; and a glance at the map will show that it was unlikely that troops at Ventersburg intended to overtake me in a hurry at Lindley would be sent to the latter place viâ Kroonstad.

In the same bundle of telegrams I found one from the Commandant at Rail-head, telling me of the departure of the convoy which had been captured.

Our interests at this time were chiefly centred on supplies, which were, to say the least of it, uncertain. The telegraph line had long been cut, too far off to mend, and, although Browne had got into heliographic communication with Vredefort, the sky was generally cloudy, and for several days we could not signal. As early as the 11th all local supplies were exhausted, and the question of how to feed the inhabitants had been a serious one. On that day I had two heliograph messages from the Chief of the Staff, the first saying that De Wet, with 3,600 men and five guns, had destroyed the Rhenoster and Leeuw Spruit bridges on the railway; and the second, that there was a rumour that Botha had retaken Kroonstad, and that I should be careful to eke out my supplies as long as possible; he added that if the rumour were true, of which he would inform me, I should have to move on the railway. As it turned out, the rumour proved to be false, and we had not to move; but had we been obliged to do so, what to do with the sick would have been a serious question. As soon as I got to Heilbron, I began to send off Hamilton's sick and wounded under the Red Cross, but we had still a hundred of our own left, of whom the P.M.O. reported sixty as unfit to move, and I therefore telegraphed to the Chief of the Staff that, if we had to leave them behind, the inhabitants could not supply them, as they had hardly enough for themselves.

On the 18th we had only one day's half-rations left, and I had just settled that, unless something turned up, I should march out next morning and fight my way to the railway, when I had a message from Methuen saying that he was bringing a convoy from Vredefort next day, and asking me to help him by making a demonstration towards Eland's Kop. I thought that if the Boers opposed him there I could not help better than by shelling them in rear. Grant was therefore ordered to take his guns along the Vredefort road, and a battalion of the Highland Brigade, with the Eastern Province Horse and Lovat's Scouts, detailed as escort. Next morning Grant found an excellent position between 10,000 and 11,000 yards to the south-east of Eland's Kop, and remained in it, his front covered by the Seaforth. While he was doing this I had a heliograph message from Methuen, saying that he had found the enemy in such force that he could not get on without his other brigade, which he had sent for, and should attack next day. He rather reproachfully said that surely I might have made a demonstration. Almost at the moment I was reading this Grant had espied a large body of Boers in a hollow on the south side of the hills, close together, and unaware that there were any English nearer to them than Methuen's men on the other side of the ridge. This belief, however, Grant soon shattered, for his first shot landed fair into the middle of them, and almost before he could get his second round in they had scattered all over the plain. They evidently did not like these six-mile shots from the rear, for they never came back, and half an hour afterwards Methuen marched through unopposed, and thanked me for the help we had given him. The convoy was taken over by the Seaforth, and he moved off to the northwards.

This ended our supply difficulties, for before we ran short again the railway was opened to Heilbron.

This convoy brought us some mails—a luxury we had not had since we left Winburg—and also a long memorandum by Lord Roberts, saying that, in order to insure the security of the railway and to establish order in the north-eastern district of the Orange River Colony, it was necessary not only to provide adequate garrisons for the principal towns and vulnerable points of the railway, but also to organize flying columns which should be constantly on the move through the various districts where the burghers were still in arms against us. A detail of these columns then followed, the Highland Brigade, with the Eastern Province Horse, six companies of

Yeomanry, and a battery of Field Artillery, under command of Macdonald, forming one of them.

This order left me, with a full Divisional Staff, to command Grant's men with the two Naval guns, and as this seemed too like Bon Gaultier's 'four-and-twenty men and five-and-thirty pipers' to be seriously intended, I telegraphed to the Military Secretary, saying I supposed that I and the Staff of the Ninth Division were not to remain at Heilbron. On the 20th I had an answer, numbered C. 2,165, saying that we were to do so for the present. We all wondered what use, if any, we should be put to there, but got no further information on the subject till the 26th, when I had another telegram from the Military Secretary, saying:

'Please cancel my telegram, C. 2165 of 20 June and act on that of C. of S. of the same date.'

As I had not received any telegram from the Chief of the Staff of that date, I ordered a search to be made, but found that no such telegram had been received at either the telegraph or heliograph stations, so telegraphed asking that it might be repeated. In answer I had the following on the 28th:

'PRETORIA,

'No. 340, 27th June.—Your 209 to Military Secretary C. 2316 as follows Leave your A.A.G. at Heilbron and come here with the remainder of your Staff.—C.O.S.'

A train was due that evening, so I asked the Railway Staff Officer to arrange that when it returned it should take us through to Pretoria. This could not be definitely settled till the train came in, as officers, servants, grooms, horses, waggons, etc., took a good deal of room; but we found that the train which came would just hold us, and at half-past eight we moved off. The Highlanders had left that morning, and practically the division was broken up; but I suppose anything is in being as long as its head is alive, and the Staff was still together, except poor Ewart, whom we left, looking very doleful, on the platform.

At nine next morning we reached Pretoria, and after breakfast I reported myself to Lord Roberts. What he and I said to each other has nothing to do with the story of the Ninth Division. I have often dwelt, maybe at tedious length, on my own thoughts and motives, as it was on these that the division moved, and for some of which it had to suffer; but henceforth these affected no one but myself: suffice it therefore to say that he showed thorough disapproval of my work, and gave no hint that he valued that of the division, which he said was broken up.

I lunched with some of the Headquarter Staff, and dined with all my own. Next morning Murray and I left by the nine o'clock train for Cape Town.

The Nineteenth Brigade was on the Line of Communications; the Highland Brigade, the Eastern Province Horse, the Engineer company, and the

Field Battery, formed parts of the group of flying columns. Grant and his men of the Naval Brigade stayed at Heilbron, and my Staff stood together for the last time on the Pretoria Station platform. The Ninth Division was at an end. In view of after-events, it cannot be truly said, 'Its end was peace.'

APPENDICES

APPENDIX I

Staff Chief Officer's Time-Table of Sannah's Post Affair, 31st March, 1900.

Left Bloemfontein	5.30 a.m.
General Colvile reached Bushman's Kop with his Staff	11.15 a.m.
General Macdonald, leading Highland Brigade, arrived abreast of Bushman's Kop	11.40 a.m.
The rear part of Division did not close up till past noon to Bushman's Kop	

Message sent by General Colvile to Chief of Staff at 11.35 a.m.

'Broadwood was attacked last night at Waterworks, and retired this morning with considerable loss. It is reported that all his baggage and some of his guns are in the hands of the enemy. My infantry will be here shortly, when I shall advance, leaving detachment to hold this position. Fuller report after seeing Broadwood. Enemy is in possession of Waterworks.

'Colvile, Bushman's Kop.'

Captain Ruggles-Brise was sent to General Broadwood, and was some time looking for him.

MESSAGE TO GENERAL COLVILE FROM CHIEF OF STAFF;
TIME 12.15 P.M. ON MESSAGE.

'You should push on your Mounted Infantry and guns, and do all you can to assist Broadwood, and clear this side of SPRUITKOP as informed.'

(*Note.*—The M.I. were at Waterval under Henry, and had been there before General Colvile's arrival.)

At 12.40 p.m. General Colvile issued orders for turning movement viâ Waterval Drift, and at 1 p.m. Division was moving.

3.25 p.m. Highland Brigade hotly engaged.

MESSAGE RECEIVED 3.28 P.M. FROM LORD ROBERTS TO
LIEUTENANT-GENERAL COLVILE.

'The enemy will endeavour to delay you in spruit to give themselves time to carry off the guns. It is very desirable, therefore, that you should, if possible, make a turning movement which will enable you to act on their line of retreat. French's Cavalry Brigade, which should shortly be with you, will help to this end. Acknowledge receipt of this.'

MESSAGE SENT 4.10 P.M. BY GENERAL COLVILE TO
CHIEF OF THE STAFF.

'I am making turning movement by a point North of Waterval Drift. Found myself opposed at Waterval Drift, and therefore extended my turning movement. About 10,000 of the enemy at Likat Long.'

General Colvile arrived Waterval Drift at 6 p.m.

APPENDIX I

MESSAGE THEN SENT TO CHIEF OF STAFF.

'Have arrived at Waterval Drift, whence I shall try to cut off enemy, but have no cavalry to-day, as Broadwood is incapable of moving. He has lost 8 guns. Enemy with guns holding spruit between Waterval and Waterworks.'

During the night all transport of Ninth Division was passed over Waterval Drift.

MESSAGE FROM GENERAL FRENCH RECEIVED AFTER DARK FROM BUSHMAN'S KOP.

'*To General Colvile.*

'I will be with you at 6 A.M. to-morrow.'

LATER MESSAGE FROM GENERAL COLVILE TO CHIEF OF STAFF.

'French halted for night at Bushman's Kop; shall await his arrival in the morning before advancing further. I had about 6 casualties. Broadwood tells me he has reported to you direct. River and kopjes for about 4 miles North of this have been cleared of enemy, who now holds Maliko in force.

'Two very large laagers visible.'

MESSAGE TO GENERAL COLVILE (THROUGH GENERAL FRENCH) RECEIVED ABOUT 7.30 P.M., AND DESPATCHED 6.15 P.M.

'A 640. If the enemy are as strong as you have reason to believe at Likat Long, it would be better for you with your whole Division to fall back on Boesman's Kop, otherwise it is not impossible they may try to cut off your communications with Bloemfontein by turning your right flank.

'Communicate this to French, and acknowledge receipt. The force with which Broadwood has been engaged is under De Wet, and came from Brandfort, and, crossing the Modder River at Kranz Kraal, got right in his rear during the night. He will probably try the same game with you, when you will probably be between two fires. Acknowledge receipt.'

From General Colvile to Chief of Staff in Reply.

'Your A 640 just received. I cannot get my transport back over the drift in the dark. I proposed to turn De Wet's right flank, but will review situation carefully by daylight. If De Wet tries to turn my right flank, he will find himself in very favourable ground for French, who should be able to get at him. If worst comes to the worst, I do not think he can prevent me falling back on Tucker. I left four companies at Bushman's Kop.

'COLVILE (midnight).

April 1st.

To Chief of Staff.

'Enemy has been reinforced during the night. Four laagers are now visible. He shows no disposition to move, and is probably waiting to see what I do. My Division is numerically only equal to a strong Brigade and I am not strong enough to leave a sufficient containing force and make a flank movement, which would seriously threaten his communications. I shall thoroughly reconnoitre his position to-day, but unless I find him much weaker than I imagine, or receive orders to the contrary, I propose to

APPENDIX I

withdraw my transport over the drift at dusk and retire on Bushman's Kop. French, who was due here at 6 A.M., has not arrived, and I can see no signs of him.

'COLVILE, 7.45 A.M.'

General French arrived at 10.30 a.m. on April 1st at Waterval Drift.

MESSAGE FROM MILITARY SECRETARY, 12.15 P.M.

'April 1st, 787: In reply to yours of this date to C of S. Your proposal is approved. Do not engage enemy, as you are not strong enough to do so with advantage. Act as you propose by sending transport to drift after dusk and retire on Bushman's Kop. Keep Knox informed.'

APPENDIX II

A

ARMY HEADQUARTERS,
BLOEMFONTEIN,
25*th April*, 1900.

To G.O.C. NINTH DIVISION.

The following extract from a despatch, dated the 20th April, 1900, from Brigadier-General Broadwood, commanding 2nd Cavalry Brigade, describing the engagement at Sannah's Post on the 31st March, is forwarded for any remarks you may wish to make, more particularly as regards your reasons for not advancing from Boesman's Kop to the assistance of the Cavalry Brigade.

By order,
H. V. COWAN,
Lieutenant-Colonel,
Military Secretary.

Extract.

'9. About noon a Staff officer arrived from the G.O.C. 9th Division to say he had reached Boesman's Kop. I suggested that a direct advance on the spruit offered the best chance of assisting. About 2 p.m. I was informed that the 9th Division had moved towards Waterval Drift; so seeing any hope of recapturing the guns at an end, I began sending

APPENDIX II

the units to their camps, the Mounted Infantry and guns to Bloemfontein, and the cavalry to Springfield, as, owing to the loss of the baggage, it was inadvisable to bivouac where we were.'

B

MILITARY SECRETARY.

With reference to the extract from Brigadier-General Broadwood's despatch of the 20th April, 1900, given in your memorandum of the 25th April, 1900, the statements in that extract do not agree with the facts as reported to me.

On hearing, at Springfield, of the reverse of Brigadier-General Broadwood's Brigade, between the Waterworks and Boesman's Kop, I ordered Lieutenant-Colonel Flint to push on with his Brigade Division; and hastened myself to Boesman's Kop, where I found Lieutenant-Colonel Martyr, by whom I was informed that Brigadier-General Broadwood's Brigade was then forming up about two miles to the eastward. I at once sent my D.A.A.G., Captain Ruggles-Brise, to Brigadier-General Broadwood, with a message that I wished to see him, and on his return Captain Ruggles-Brise reported that Brigadier-General Broadwood had replied to this message that he was too tired to come. Under ordinary circumstances I should have taken serious notice of such an answer; but, as I gathered from Captain Ruggles-Brise that Brigadier-General Broadwood appeared to be completely broken down under the circumstances in which he found himself, and incapable of co-operation, I thought it better to let it pass. I had no intimation of the suggestion which Brigadier-General Broadwood reports that he made, 'That a direct advance on the spruit offered the best chance of assisting'; but had I received this message it would not have modified my dispositions, unless it had been backed up by some facts of which I am still in ignorance.

The position was then as follows : The Cavalry Brigade was concentrated, and safe, within two miles of Boesman's Kop; its baggage and seven R.H.A. guns were in the hands of the enemy to the east of Klip Kraal, through which the map showed an affluent of the Modder River to run, while another, and presumably smaller affluent, ran between it and Boesman's Kop. For an hour before the arrival of my infantry clouds of dust between Klip Kraal and the Waterworks showed that the enemy was busy, presumably in removing the captured guns and baggage, of which the former would obviously be taken away first. A portion of Lieut.-Colonel Martyr's Mounted Infantry was in possession of Waterval Drift, when they were being shelled by two of the enemy's guns.

Although I did not receive Brigadier-General Broadwood's suggestion, the idea of a direct advance on Klip Kraal was one that naturally offered itself; and had the Cavalry Brigade still been pressed, its reinforcement by the shortest possible route would, I consider, have been imperative; but with its safety secured the only problem before me was that of, if possible, retaking the guns. Knowing from experience that the enemy's guns generally outranged those of our Field Artillery, and seeing before me a level plain, intersected by such spruits or river beds as the enemy has frequently held for a considerable time against superior numbers, and judging that the enemy had had ample time to get the captured guns, at all events as far as the Sannah's Post Drift, it appeared to me that were I to attempt a direct advance I must undoubtedly lose heavily, and that the enemy would have every opportunity of delaying me until he got the captured guns to the eastward of the Modder River, whence he would have an unobstructed line of retreat to Thabanchu. Therefore, knowing that Waterval Drift was in our hands, I decided to effect the passage of the Modder at that point, hoping that with the aid of Lieutenant-Colonel Martyr's Mounted Infantry I might cut into the enemy's line of retreat, while with the infantry I held him in front to the north of Mamena. I accordingly ordered Lieutenant-Colonel Martyr to occupy the hills to the north of our line of march, while the Division and guns advanced on Waterval Drift, and I sent a further message to Brigadier-General Broadwood, informing him of my proposed action, and asking him to co-operate as far as the condition of his horses would permit.

As detailed in my report on these operations of the 3rd April, 1900, on approaching Waterval Drift it was found that the Mounted Infantry had been forced to abandon it, and that the enemy was in occupation of it and a hill some miles to the north on the east bank of the river. This necessitated a further turning movement and a considerable expenditure of time, with the result that it was nearly dusk before the passage of the drift was effected, and some of the troops had already done a twenty-two miles march—a state of affairs which precluded any further action for that day, even had I been strong enough, with only about 4,000 men, to hold in front the large force of the enemy which was then on the hills above the Waterworks, and detach a sufficient force to cut his line of retreat.

As we were coming into action to the west of the Waterval Drift, I received the following message from the Field-Marshal Commanding-in-Chief:

'LIEUTENANT-GENERAL COLVILE.
  'FROM FIELD-MARSHAL LORD ROBERTS,
      3.28 P.M.

'The enemy will endeavour to delay you in spruit in order to give themselves time to carry off the guns. It is very desirable, therefore, that you should, if possible, make a turning movement which will enable you to act on their line of retreat. French's Cavalry Brigade, which should shortly be with you, will help to this end. Acknowledge receipt of this.'

This information as to the speedy arrival of the cavalry more than compensated for the disappointment which the abandonment of the drift by the Mounted Infantry had caused, and I had still hopes of being able to cut into the enemy's line of retreat until hour after hour passed without any signs of them, and when at length Lieutenant-General French arrived with one brigade at 10.30 on the following morning, I agreed with him that it was too late to attempt a pursuit.

I may mention that the above-quoted message from the Field-Marshal Commanding-in-Chief appeared to me to so thoroughly sanction the line of action which I adopted, that in my report on the operations I did not consider it necessary to give my reasons for it.

I would also point out that in the verbal instructions which the Field-Marshal Commanding-in-Chief gave me before the Ninth Division left Bloemfontein he informed me that Brigadier-General Broadwood and his brigade would be under my orders; and had Brigadier-General Broadwood informed me of the reasons for his retirement on Springfield, as stated in his despatch, I should entirely have forbidden it; and I beg that I may be permitted to express my opinion that his criticism on my dispositions is highly improper.

I have explained above the reasons which then influenced me in making these dispositions, and a fuller knowledge which I have since gained of the ground and the enemy's movements, has not caused me to modify them, but my judgment may be wholly at fault, and I respectfully await the verdict of the Field-Marshal Commanding-in-Chief.

H. COLVILE,
Lieutenant-General,
Commanding Ninth Division.

Winburg,
16.5.00.

C

LIEUT.-GENERAL SIR H. COLVILE, K.C.M.G., C.B.

The F. M. C in C desires me to send you this copy of his memo^m of 21st May. The original was forwarded to you on that date.*

By order,
H. V. COWAN,
Lt Col.,
M. S.

1st July, 1900.

ARMY HEADQUARTERS,
SOUTH AFRICA, KRONSTADT,
21*st May*, 1900.

TO LIEUTENANT-GENERAL SIR H. COLVILE, K.C.M.G., ETC., ETC., COMMANDING NINTH DIVISION.

MEMO.

With reference to the attached memorandum, I am of opinion that, on his arrival at Boesman's Kop about noon on March 31st, Lieutenant-General Sir H. Colvile acted injudiciously in sending his Deputy-Assistant-Adjutant-General to summon Brigadier-General Broadwood, whose column had been seriously engaged with the enemy, and was then halted about two miles to the Eastward. If Lieutenant-General Colvile had ridden on himself to Brigadier-General Broadwood, he could have ascertained at once what the actual situation was, how he could best assist the force which he had been directed to support, and what would be the best chance of recovering the captured guns and convoy.

I am further of opinion that Brigadier-General Broadwood, who had been fighting since daybreak, and whose troops were still within striking distance of the enemy, would not have been justified in leaving his command for the purpose of communicating with Lieutenant-General

* It was not received.

Colvile. That Brigadier-General Broadwood should have been worn out, and perhaps to some extent overwhelmed, by the reverse which his column had sustained is not surprising, and on this account it was all the more necessary that Lieutenant-General Colvile should have lost no time in acquainting himself with the situation, and assuming the initiative.

Even if Brigadier-General Broadwood had complied with Lieutenant-General Colvile's order to join him at Boesman's Kop, serious delay must have occurred, as the Staff Officer from the Ninth Division had first to find Brigadier-General Broadwood, and the latter would have had to ride back and finally rejoin his troops before any concerted movement could have taken place.

By remaining inactive for some time at Boesman's Kop, and afterwards moving on Waterval Drift, Lieutenant-General Colvile gave the enemy an opportunity of removing the guns and convoy unmolested. They were not slow to avail themselves of this opportunity, and by the time the cavalry under Lieutenant-General French came up any idea of turning the enemy's flank or cutting off their retreat had to be abandoned, as during the night the Boers had rapidly retired eastwards.

ROBERTS,
Field-Marshal
Commanding-in-Chief, South Africa.

D

(Sent to the Military Secretary, War Office, London, on Receipt of C.)

MEMO.

With reference to the attached memorandum from Field-Marshal Lord Roberts, a perfect view of the surrounding country and of the enemy was obtainable from Boesman's Kop, which was not the case from the position

APPENDIX II

in which Brigadier-General Broadwood was halted, and I maintain that the general situation could be far better ascertained from the former than from the latter place.

Brigadier-General Broadwood halted at a spot four miles from the nearest of the enemy (who were retiring when I arrived), and two miles from Boesman's Kop.

As my Staff officer returned to Boesman's Kop, after seeing Brigadier-General Broadwood, before the arrival of the infantry of the Ninth Division, Brigadier-General Broadwood, had he accompanied him, would also have arrived before it, and no delay would have occurred.

On the evidence of Major Burnham, the scout who was taken prisoner at Klip Kraal, the last of Brigadier-General Broadwood's guns had been taken across the Modder River, near the Waterworks, by 12 noon, and the enemy's retirement was continued till 4 p.m., when a halt was made for the night. As I did not arrive at Boesman's Kop till 11.15, and the Division about half an hour after me, the enemy had eight miles start, which I had no chance of lessening until they halted.

Had the cavalry under Lieutenant-General French arrived at the time indicated in Lord Roberts' telegram quoted in my memo, they would have been able to overtake the enemy at his halting-place. Having marched twenty-one miles, my Division could not have continued its march to that place, but they could have pushed on a few more miles in support of the cavalry.

There was no inactivity at Boesman's Kop, except a necessary halt for the troops, after a thirteen-miles march.

H. E. COLVILE,
Major-General.

31.7.00.

APPENDIX III

EXTRACT FROM ARMY ACT.

Redress of Wrongs.

Mode of Complaint by Officer.
'42. If an officer thinks himself wronged by his commanding officer, and on due application made to him does not receive the redress to which he may consider himself entitled, he may complain to the Commander-in-Chief in order to obtain justice, who is hereby required to examine into such complaint, and through a Secretary of State make his report to Her Majesty, in order to receive the directions of Her Majesty thereon.'

* * * * *

'Although the Commander-in-Chief is required to examine into the complaint and report to Her Majesty, he is not debarred from expressing his own view of the case.

'Even an expression of opinion by the intermediate general officer will in many cases suffice to render further steps unnecessary. An officer should not be disposed to push to extremes his right to bring his complaint before the Sovereign. The report to Her Majesty is to be made through the Secretary of State, the constitutional adviser of the Crown.'

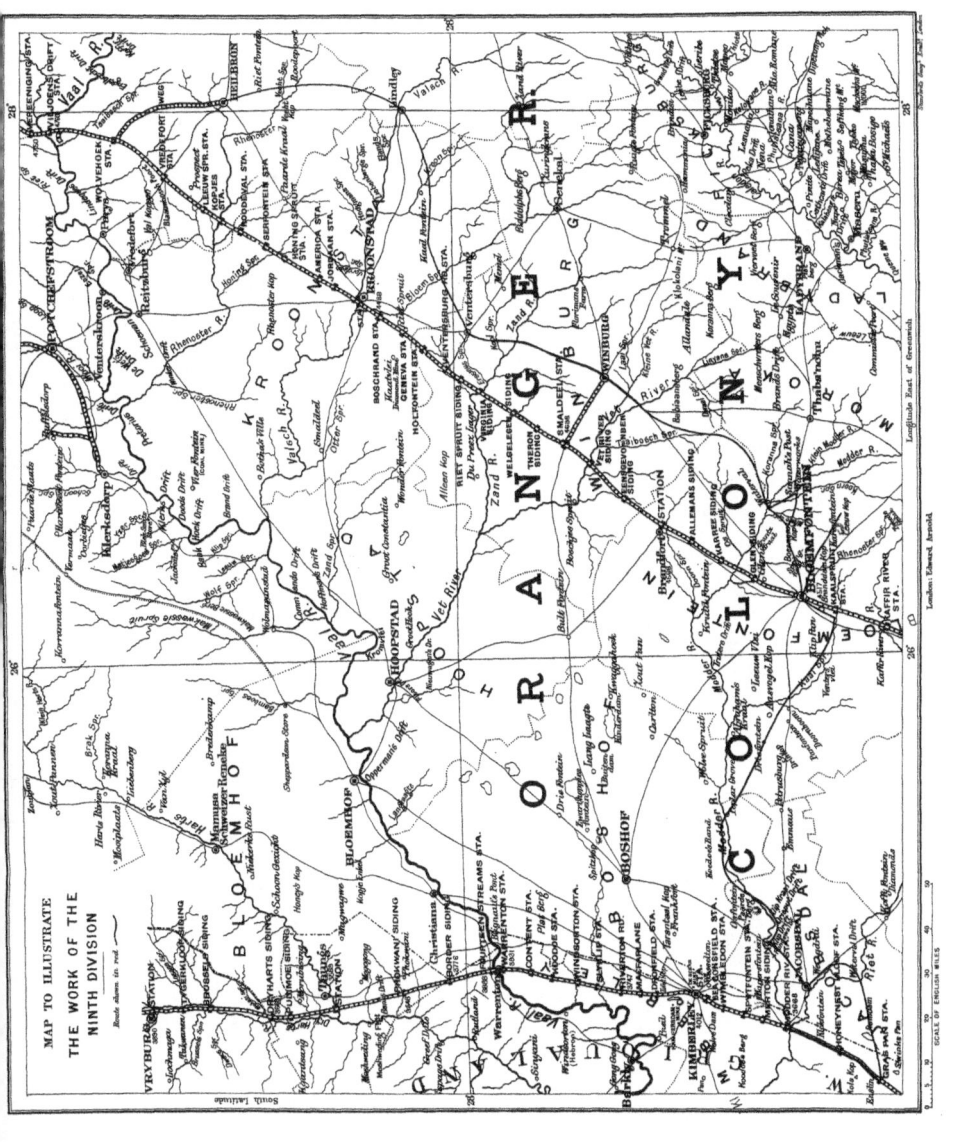

INDEX

ALDWORTH, Colonel, 39, 40
Ambulances, separation of, from convoys, 92; lack of, 119, 178
Argyll and Sutherland Highlanders —at Paardeberg, 38, 40; in reserve at Babiaansberg, 126; at Blaauwberg, 169, 170; commanding Heilbron road, 174; on Spitz Kop, 191-193, 196, 202
Army Act, extract from, on redress of wrongs, 242
Artillery fire, effects of, 194

Babiaansberg, 122-126
Barker, Colonel J. C., 19, 34, 173, 209, 210, 213
Belmont, Battle of, 2-4
Benson, Major, 11
Bertram, Lieutenant, 164, 199
Bettington, Sergeant, 200, 201
Blaauwberg, 166 and *note*, 167-169
Blaauwbosch Farm, 160
Black Watch—at Paardeberg, 38-40; at Babiaansberg, 123-126; at Blaauwberg, 168
Bloemberg, 166 *note*
Bloemfontein, arrival at, 66; Waterworks not considered essential to, 90 and *note*; scheme for defence of, ordered by Lord Roberts, 94; return to, 97
Blue Hill, 62, 63
Boers, practical character of, 42; courage of, 51; wounded well treated by, 92; white flag abused by, 162 *note*; tactics of, 171
Boesman's Kop, Broadwood's engagement near, 69-72, 74; observations from, 82; Kitchener advises retirement on, 88, 89; retirement effected, 92; message sent to Hamilton from, 104; telegraph terminus at, 107; Highland Light Infantry arrives at, 113

Boots, lack of, 67, 95
Brabant, General, supplies awaited by, 147, 149, 151, 153, 154
Bradshaw, Quartermaster, 150, 152, 153
Broadwood, Gen., retirement and reverse of, at Waterworks, 68-70, 73, 74, 79 *note*; sent for, to Boesman's Kop, 77; answer returned by, 81; view of, regarding direct advance, 82, 83; despatch of, 139, 140, 234; reply to, 235-238
Browne, Lieutenant A. N. E., 19, 61, 123
Burnham, Major, 87, 88 *note*

Cactus Hill, 60
Campbell, Lieutenant Hon. R., 19, 66, 155
Canadians—at Paardeberg, 36, 38, 40, 47; Lieutenant McLean supplied from, 45; at Poplar Grove, 58; enteric prevalent among, 98
Carthew-Yorstoun, Colonel, 124, 126, 179
Cavalry, relations of, with Chief of Staff, 96
City Imperial Volunteers at Ramdam, 23
Clements, General, 157
Cloete, Lieutenant, 138, 139
Clothing, insufficiency of, 67, 111, 156
Codrington, Lieutenant-Colonel, 8
Coldstream Guards—at Belmont, 4; at Modder River, 6, 8, 10; retirement of, from Magersfontein, 16
Column, length of, on march to Lindley, 158 *note*
Complaint by an officer, mode of, 242
Connacher, Surgeon, given back by President Steyn, 218, 219

16—2

Convoy from Roodevaal, despatch and loss of, 216-219
Cornwalls. See Duke of Cornwall's
Correspondence regarding Broadwood, 234-241
Cowan, Colonel, letter to, regarding Hamilton's command, 135
Cronje, Commandant, offers surrender at Paardeberg, 42; surrenders, 50
Cuthbertson, Major, 98, 138, 209

Daily Telegraph cited, 88 *note*
De Rust's Farm, 179
De Wet, Commandant Christian, between Lindley and Heilbron, 172, 173, 198; on railway near Rhenoster, 222, 223
De Wet, Commandant P., 198
Divisional Staff, members of, 18
Doornboom, 65
Dorman, Lieutenant-Colonel J. C., 19, 91, 98, 138
Douglas, General, 222
Dreifontein, 65
Duke of Cornwall's Light Infantry at Paardeberg, 39, 40; at Sannah's Post, 85

Eastern Province Horse detailed for escort to Pole-Carew, 97; condition of, 113, 119, 121; patrol of, captured, 141-143; dwindling of, 158, 164, 169, 170 *note*, 197
Elliot Wood, General, 46
Enslin, fight at, 5
Enteric fever, water not the only cause of, 24; prevalence of, at Bloemfontein, 67; Nineteenth Brigade severely attacked by, 98; Divisional Staff attacked by, 138, 155
Ewart, Lieutenant-Colonel E. S., appointed A.A.G., 18; hard work of, 26; encounters obstructive sentry, 209; at Paardeberg, 39, 40, 51; makes flag for Headquarters, 45; down with fever, 138; recovered, 154; thrown by his horse, 165; remains at Heilbron, 227

Fererra's Spruit, 65
Fielding, Captain, 8
Flag, construction of, 45
Flint, Colonel, 70, 83, 84

French, General, at Boesman's Kop, 88; arrives at Waterval Drift, 90; proposes march on Dewetsdorp, 106

Germiston, 214
Gleichen, Major A. E. W. Count, 19, 45, 50, 96, 122, 173, 187, 188, 198, 209, 210
Gleichen's Horse, 179, 201
Gordon Highlanders, 36, 47
Grant's naval guns, 23, 26, 78, 123, 125, 167, 168, 193, 203, 205-208, 224, 228
Graspan, fight at, 5
Grenadier Guards at Belmont, 4; at Modder River, 6, 10; retirement from Magersfontein, 16, 17
Groetfontein, 106
Groot Krantz Drift, 180
Gun, capture of, at Leeuwkop, 64
Gun Hill, 36

Hamilton, Major-General Ian, Waterworks held by, 104; message to, from Boesman's Kop, 104; from Klip Kraal, 105; goes to Thaba 'Nchu, 107; bivouacs at Verkerdes Vlei, 119; Winburg and Babiaansberg, 120-133; awkwardness of position in regard to, 133-136; in need of supplies, 137; appoints Landdrost, 138; meets severe opposition at Roodepoort, 200; sick left at Heilbron by, 212, 223
Hamman's Spruit, 166
Hats for helmets, 160
Heilbron, march to, ordered, 146; exact orders issued for march, 175; course of march, 176 *et seq.;* one-third rations during march, 184; arrival at, 209
Henry, Colonel, 62, 84, 96
Highland Brigade at Magersfontein, 13-15; at Ramdam, 23; march to Klip Kraal, 31, 32; at Paardeberg, 36-40, 50; at Poplar Grove, 55-58, 61-63; Sannah's Post and Waterval Drift, 78, 84, 85; ordered to Springfield, 103, 104; to Waterval Drift, 109, 115-117; at Babiaansberg, 123-126; at Blaauwberg, 168-170; skill of, 197; excellent behaviour of, 210, 211
Hopefield, 163
Horses, unfitness of, 113, 119

INDEX

Hospital, Field, lack of, 111
Huddlestone, Lieutenant, 215
Hughes - Hallett, Colonel, commands Macdonald's brigade, 39, 116; at Poplar Grove, 55, 57-59; left in command at Zand River, 157; wounded, 197, 199
Humphreys, Captain H. L., 19, 56, 138, 154

Jacobsdaal, 27
Johnson, Colonel, 102, 103

Kaalfontein, 109
Kelly-Kenny, General, Rimington's Guides with, 24; joined by Kitchener, 31; at Paardeberg, 33-38; sends separate report after Paardeberg, 52; at Poplar Grove, 65; artillery detailed from, 112; in need of supplies, 149
Kincaid, Colonel, 36, 47, 204
Kitchener, Lieutenant - General Lord, joins Kelly-Kenny, 30; orders pontoons to be left at Klip Drift, 34; Paardeberg, 35, 39; sends instructions regarding gun at Leeuwkop, 64; regarding Broadwood at the Waterworks, 83; advises retreat on Boesman's Kop, 88, 89; orders Brigade to relieve 18th, 98; censures state of transport, 99; orders march to Springfield, 103; orders forward move, 111, 112; sends instructions to follow Hamilton's Brigade, 117, 118; telegram from, regarding supplies at Winburg, 136; message to, regarding captured patrol of Eastern Province Horse, 142, 143; howitzers left at Waterworks by order of, 144; orders advance to Lindley and Ventersberg, 146; message to, from Lindley (undelivered), 178; telegram from, regarding convoy of rations, 213
Klip Drift, march to, 27-30
Klip Kraal (Koorn Spruit), Highland Brigade marches to, 31; General Porter at, 90; communications with Hamilton from, 104, 105
Kolk Liegte, 5
Koorn Spruit. See Klip Kraal
Krantz Kraal, 109, 110
Kroon Spruit, 166
Kroonstad, Headquarters at, 141

Lane, Major, 155, 172, 193, 208
Leeuwkop, 53, 54, 56, 58, 60, 62-64, 94, 96
Likatlong Hill, 87
Lindley, march to, ordered, 146; arrival at, 172
Long, Major S. S., appointed Transport officer, 19; censured, 99; superseded, 102, 103; valuable help of, 155
Looting, 28
Lovat's Scouts, 220

Macdonald, Captain, 48
Macdonald, General, at Klip Kraal, 32; at Paardeberg, 35, 39; wounded, 39, 55; at Boesman's Kop, 70; advises chase of Boers viâ Waterworks, 80, 83; ordered to retire on Boesman's Kop, 91; attempts to get supplies from Bloemfontein, 112; awkwardness in regard to authority of, 115-117, 164, 165; sent to Ventersberg, 144; in need of supplies, 149-154; suggests short route to Roode Kraal, 157; reaches Roode Kraal, 159; mounted signallers used by, 195 and *note*; at Spitz Kop, 204-207; appreciation of, 211
McLean, Lieutenant, 45, 67
McLeod, Captain, 155
Magersfontein, 13-15
Makauws Drift, 54
Mamema Hill, 87, 89, 90
Maquaastadt Farm, 163
Martyr, Colonel, at Paardeberg, 33, 34; at Boesman's Kop, 70-73, 77, 82; at Waterval Drift, 83, 96
Medical officers, lack of, 111, 159
Methuen, General Lord, opinion of, on night attacks, 2; at Belmont, 2, 3; at Modder River, 5-7, 11; at Magersfontein, 13, 15; sent to help Ninth Division, 199, 215; goes to Lindley to relieve Yeomanry, 215; brings convoy from Vredefort, 224
Modder River, Battle of, 5-11; crossed four times, 101 *note*
Morago, Smith-Dorrien's move on, 109, 112, 114
Morning Post cited, 58
Mules, unfitness of, 21, 69, 99-103
Murray, Lord George, 67, 155, 227

Netley, Commandant, 198
Night attacks, 2; marching, 25

Ninth Division, composition of, 18
Nugent, Captain George, 1, 12, 17, 18, 52, 128, 155

Oliver, Commandant, 198
Osfontein, 52, 53
Outpost Kopje, 55
Ox transport, loss of, at the Riet River, 26; bad state of oxen, 181

Paget, Gen. Arthur, 6, 11, 12
Papjes Valley, 119
Paarde Kraal, 97
Paardeberg, operations at, 33-51; half-rations at, 184; Sergeant Bettington at, 201
Pigott, Captain, 137, 138, 152, 155
Pole-Carew, General, 5, 10, 11
Pom-poms, 8-10
Poplar Grove, 53-64, 96
Porter, General, 90-92, 96
Potgieter, Commandant, 171-173
Pretoria, interview with Lord Roberts at, 227
Prinsloo, Commandant, 171, 173

Queen's Birthday, observation of, 161

Ramdam, 20, 23
Rations, scarcity of. See Supplies
Raymond, Lieutenant H. E., 19, 209
Redress of wrongs, extract from Army Act regarding, 242
Remount Depot, unfitness of animals supplied by, 102
Rhenoster River, 180, 193 *note*; bridge destroyed by De Wet, 223
Riet River, 7, 8, 25, 26, 101 *note*
Rietfontein (near Bloemfontein), 95, 97
Rietfontein (near Spitz Kop), 206
Rimington's Guides, 24
Roberts, Field-Marshal Lord, night marching advised by, 25; 'suitable escort' defined by, 26; orders march to Kimberley, 27; discourages looting, 28; arrives at Paardeberg, 42; averse to an assault, 46; approves of attack made, 51; details force for Poplar Grove, 53; issues orders regarding Broadwood at Waterworks, 68, 84; promises French as support, 84; instructs Hamilton regarding occupation of Waterworks, 90 *note*; approves action of Ninth Division regarding Sannah's Post, 93; orders scheme for defence of Bloemfontein, 94; issues instructions regarding support of Hamilton and Smith-Dorrien, 104; telegram sent by, from Smalldeel, 132; correspondence with, regarding Broadwood affair, 141, 237-240; interview with, 227
Robertson, Rev. J., 19
Roode Kraal, 157-159
Roodepoort, 191-203
Roodevaal, railhead at, 214
Rous, Mr., 209, 214
Ruggles-Brise, Captain, starts for South Africa, 1; appointed D.A.A.G., 18; hard work of, 26; takes messages to Broadwood, 73 *note*, 77, 78, 83; brings reply, 81, 82; joins staff of Eleventh Division, 98
Rundle, General, French goes in support of, 106; supplies awaited by, 147, 149, 151, 153, 154
Rustfontein, 196, 204

Sannah's Post, operations at, 68-93; supply depôt for Thaba 'Nchu district, 108
Scots Guards—at Belmont, 4; at Modder River, 6-8, 10; at Magersfontein, 14; retirement from Magersfontein, 16
Seaforth Highlanders—at Paardeberg, 38-40; at Babiaansberg, 123, 126; at Blaauwberg, 169; at Roodepoort, 192, 196, 202
Senekal, 141, 142
Sentries' obstructions, 29, 30
Shropshires—at Paardeberg, 36, 46; gun taken by, at Leeuwkop, 63
Signallers, mounted, lack of, 61, 195
Slagtlaagte, 64
Smalldeel, 132
Smith-Dorrien, General, at Gras Pan, 20; encounters obstructive sentry, 30; at Paardeberg, 36, 41, 43, 47; at Leeuwkop, 54, 55, 57-59, 62-64; opinion of, regarding Broadwood's guns, 78, 81, 83; at Waterval Drift, 84; ordered to relieve Eighteenth Brigade, 98; goes to Thaba 'Nchu, 107; moves on Morago, 109, 112, 114

INDEX

Spitz Kop, situation of, 166, 180; Highlanders on, 191-193, 196, 202; Boers fire from, 205, 207
Spragge, Colonel, note from, 181-185; reply to, 188; misleading telegram received by, 188, 189; Methuen goes to relief of, 215
Springfield, guns heard near, 69; halt at, 93; cavalry return to, 97; order for advance to, 98; march from, ordered, 108
Steinkamp, Commandant, 198
Steyn, Mr. John, 65, 66
Steyn, President, reported east of New York, 119; orders removal of white flags from farms, 162 *note;* Heilbron inhabitants loyal to, 214; Surgeon Connacher returned by, 218
Supplies, Kitchener's instructions regarding, at Winburg, 136; scarcity of, 137, 138 and *note,* 149-151, 212, 213, 217, 220, 221, 223, 224
Susannafontein, 127

Telegraph instrument, lack of, 121, 173
Thaba 'Nchu, Hamilton and Smith-Dorrien sent to, 107
Three Stone Hill, 57
Transport, loss of, at Riet River, 26; censure on state of, 99
Trenches of Boers, shape of, at Paardeberg, 42, 43
Tweefontein Farm, 166

Urmston, Major, 38, 169, 174
Valsch River, 174
Van Zyl, Mr., 138, 139
Vecht Kop, 202, 204
Vecht Spruit, 193 and *note,* 194, 196, 202
Ventersberg, hospital and clothes supplied at, 111, 112; move on, ordered, 145; eccentric inhabitant of, 159; telegram from Kitchener sent by General Douglas to, 222
Ventersvlei, 65
Verkerdes Vlei, 119
Vet River, 128, 129

Waterval Drift, march to, ordered, 68, 69, 73, 74, 81; advantages of route, 76, 77; Martyr's operations at, 83; march to (30th April), 111; orders issued for march, 116
Waterworks Drift, condition of, 86; crossed by Hamilton, 107
Wauchope, General, 14
Wegdrai Drift, 27
Welkom Drift, 128
Wigham, Captain, 112, 158
Winburg, movement on, 120-133
White flag on farms, 162 *note*
Wood, General Elliot, 46

Yeomanry, delay of, 158, 159, 170, 190 *note.* See also Spragge

Zand River, supplies to come from, 150-154; arrival at, 157

THE END

www.ingramcontent.com/pod-product-compliance
Lightning Source LLC
Chambersburg PA
CBHW031137160426
43193CB00008B/171